PRAISE FOR *LE*

CH00735278

"At the heart of great leadersh
Lead The Room, Shane brings
with infectious energy and enthusiasm. Shane's personal
relatable, story-driven style means you can't help but enjoy this
book. More than that, no matter where you are in your leadership journey, you can't help but learn from it."

– Tim Costello, Chief Advocate, World Vision Australia

"We don't need more eloquent speakers we need more authentic communicators. We need to give more focus to our character and content than we do our form and delivery. Thank you, Shane, for providing a tool to encourage that."

– Daniel Flynn, Co-founder Thankyou and best-selling author of *Chapter One*

"This is the best Australian book on leadership and speaking that I have ever read. Taking a topic that scares most people, Shane creates a model to help people succeed in leading a team, the room, a conference facility and probably even the MCG. It is easy reading, if you want to be a great leader then this book is guaranteed to help."

– Toby Hall, Group CEO, St Vincent's Health Australia

"In a noisy world where people are constantly challenged with how to grab attention to deliver important messages to gain essential engagement and positioning, leadership matters more than ever. This book is smart, written by a credible leader, packaged in a way that shows you why, what and how. Don't delay – study this, action this and lead the room powerfully."

– Christina Guidotti, CEO, Leading Women

"*Lead the Room* uses easy-to-understand models and concepts to illustrate the interconnection between leadership and communication. The personalised narrative compels you to want to be a better leader and the practical techniques give you a process to be a better communicator. The book is a wonderful blend of intellect and emotion, both in the way it is told and the content that is covered. Both emerging and experienced leaders will benefit from reading this."

– Rachel Tulia, Head of People & Culture, Department of Treasury and Finance Victoria

"Shane's book is a refreshing and necessary read in a world where many leaders are struggling to connect their messages with the people they lead. This book genuinely connected with me as a CEO leading transformation. Shane beautifully articulates 'When you lead with a desire to add value for the people you are speaking to, you demonstrate that you value them. You tell them you care about their time, you appreciate that they showed up and you want to leave them in a better place than where you found them.' What leader would not want to strive for this? This book will be one that I continue to use as a leader and one that I purchase for those that I coach."

– Leanne Williams, CEO, West Gippsland Libraries

"For leaders to be seen and heard they don't just need to know how to build a platform they also need to know how to lead from it. Great leaders speak into the hearts and minds of the people they care for. In *Lead the Room* Shane shows you how."

– Matt Church, Founder, Thought Leaders Global, Voted Top 10 Conference Speakers Globally

LEAD
THE

Communicate
a message
that *counts*
in moments
that *matter*

ROOM

SHANE MICHAEL HATTON

*To my beloved wife Cassandra who inspires me
not just to be a better leader but to be a better human.*

*To my big beautiful family, both by blood and choice,
who love, support and celebrate with me.*

*To every leader who has taken the time to see and
draw out the potential inside of me that at times
I could not see in myself.*

*To the many brilliant people, whose names
could fill a book of their own, who have helped shape the
experiences and wisdom contained in these pages.*

My deepest and most heartfelt, thank you.

First published in 2019 by Major Street Publishing Pty Ltd. Reprinted in 2022.
PO Box 106, Highett, Vic. 3190
E: info@majorstreet.com.au
W: majorstreet.com.au
M: +61 421 707 983

Quantity sales. Special discounts are available on quantity purchases by corporations, associations and others. For details, contact Lesley Williams using the contact details above.

Individual sales. Major Street publications are available through most bookstores. They can also be ordered directly from Major Street's online bookstore at www.majorstreet.com.au.

Orders for university textbook/course adoption use. For orders of this nature, please contact Lesley Williams using the contact details above.

The moral rights of the author have been asserted.

NATIONAL LIBRARY OF AUSTRALIA

A catalogue record for this book is available from the National Library of Australia

ISBN: 978-0-6484795-2-9

Cover design by Simone Geary
Internal design by Production Works
Printed in Australia by Ovato, an Accredited ISO AS/NZS 14001:2004 Environmental Management System Printer.

10 9 8 7 6 5 4 3 2

Disclaimer: The material in this publication is in the nature of general comment only, and neither purports nor intends to be advice. Readers should not act on the basis of any matter in this publication without considering (and if appropriate taking) professional advice with due regard to their own particular circumstances. The author and publisher expressly disclaim all and any liability to any person, whether a purchaser of this publication or not, in respect of anything and the consequences of anything done or omitted to be done by any such person in reliance, whether whole or partial, upon the whole or any part of the contents of this publication.

CONTENTS

PREFACE

Have you noticed how many of our greatest achievements in life are born of moments of deep uncertainty? That sinking feeling you get as you stand at the base of the mountain. *Can I do this? Have I got what it takes?* For many, the fear of the climb pulls them back into the comfort and safety of the familiar. But I know this: only those who *decide* to challenge this uncertainty, to take that next step forward, experience the elation of a new perspective, the thrill of success and the joy of completion that are the rewards of conquering their mountain. And in time they look back at the mountain that once towered over them, and they wonder why they had hesitated even for a moment.

What has been one of your biggest achievements? Graduating from university, getting married and buying our first home would be strong contenders for me. One of my biggest achievements, though, occurred in April 2013. To understand this achievement we need to rewind to the middle of 2012. My wife Cassandra and I had just sat down for dinner in front of the TV (don't judge us). While I jumped right into the meal Cassandra sat there silently and gave me a look. We had been married for about four and a half years, so I was by no means an expert on marriage, but I did know what it meant when she gave me *that* look. It meant she wanted to talk about something important. Of course my instinctive response was to reel through all the things I might have missed, done or, worse, not done. Did she get a haircut? Did I take the bins out? Oh gosh, what did I just say?

As I cautiously slipped in another mouthful she said, 'I think we should go to Paris for our fifth wedding anniversary...'

I felt relieved, excited and nervous in equal measure. Relieved that I hadn't done anything wrong, excited about the possibility of going to Europe and nervous for our poor little bank account.

'That's a brilliant idea. I'm all for it!' was my response. I knew better and should have let her finish.

'We should run the Paris marathon with your dad,' she declared.

I looked down past the crumbs on my stomach to the uneaten food on my plate and felt a formless sense of terror at the very thought of running a marathon.

'It's only 42.195 kilometres,' she laughed.

I discreetly dusted myself off and responded carefully, 'I'm more of a wine-and-cheese than a running kind of guy really'.

While she sat there dreamily imagining running through the beautiful streets of Paris, my mind couldn't help but jump to all the YouTube videos I've seen of runners losing control of their bodily functions and getting carried away by paramedics.

I'm not a runner.

I couldn't do a marathon.

Where would I even start?

How do you prepare for a marathon?

I'm tired out just thinking about it.

At that time I struggled to run for five minutes without medical attention and here was my wife expecting me to run for more than five hours.

Yet the concept excited me too. The idea of finishing a marathon inspired me, but the journey seemed utterly unattainable from where I was sitting.

Maybe you've decided you want to be an influential leader. You want to make a difference when you stand up to speak. You want to lead and mobilise your team around your vision, to navigate uncertainty, and to build and strengthen your culture. The concept excites you, but the journey to get there just seems beyond your reach from where you are right now.

You think about the last time you had an opportunity to speak and remember how you felt like you had lost control of your bodily functions: you started sweating and shaking, your heart pounded and you felt sick.

Have you ever said or thought:

I'm not a speaker.

I don't do public speaking.

I'm an introvert, so public speaking isn't my thing.

Where would I even start?

How do I get my thoughts down on paper? How do I prepare?

You aren't alone. Around 74 per cent of people experience some form of speech anxiety when it comes to speaking in public. A study undertaken by software company Prezi found that 75 per cent of respondents wanted to get better at presenting and 70 per cent said it was critical to their job.

We know this matters, but let's be real, that doesn't make it easy.

I've delivered many workshops on this topic. Early on I ask people to write a list of as many answers as possible to the question 'What scares you about speaking in public?' I've heard some interesting responses. Do any of these sound familiar?

What if I look like an idiot or make a fool of myself?
What if I forget what to say or go blank?
What if people laugh at me?
I feel sick in my stomach, can't stop sweating and my hands keep shaking.

But when we take time to dig a little deeper, what people are really saying is:

What if I lose the respect of my leadership, peers or team?
What if people think I'm not very good at my job?
What if people think I'm not a good leader?
What if people think I'm just no good?

In all the workshops I've delivered I have yet to hear a response to this question that shocks or even surprises me. I've heard them all and have found they can all be boiled down to two main obstacles:

- lack of confidence
- lack of clarity.

It's normal to lack confidence if you haven't had the opportunity to speak regularly. When was the last time you felt confident at something from the first time you did it? It's also perfectly normal to lack confidence if you have tried something and it didn't work the way you expected.

I have been working hard my entire life to get past my fear of flying. This last year I have had to fly more than 60 times, which has helped. And while I have mostly dealt with my lack of confidence with flying, every now and then I have an unusually bumpy flight that shakes my confidence and I feel like I'm back at the start. The key is to not stop flying!

If you're like me and are situated towards the introverted end of the spectrum, it's also pretty easy to get caught up in the self-fulfilling prophecy that robs our confidence. A research report titled 'The Effects of Speaker Personality on Anticipated Reactions to Public Speaking' explores this idea:

> *'Introverts appear less willing to speak and are more prone to public speaking anxiety. They also expect more negative evaluations from the audience and show greater fear of generating a negative opinion of themselves among the audience members. This may lead to a self-fulfilling prophecy because those who are more reluctant to speak are generally evaluated less favourably by audience members.'*
> (Macintyre & Thivierge, 1995)

For some people I work with, confidence isn't an issue (and they are the first to tell me so). They have no issues standing in front of a crowd, big or small. What I often hear these people say is they want to connect more. They want people to 'get' what they have to say. They want to say more in fewer words and say something that people actually remember. Their main issue is they can't get clarity on where to start, how to do it and how to get the whirlwind of thoughts racing around in their head organised enough to communicate to others.

Our world is changing rapidly. We are in the middle of the greatest technological shift since the industrial revolution. Recently I watched an online video of Google's personal assistant making a phone call to a hair salon to book an appointment on a person's behalf. The future is wildly unpredictable and exciting, but one thing technology will never be able to replicate is the value of soft skills like communication and personal connection. That said, I've learned that it takes a lot of effort to make something look effortless. Those soft skills are actually hard work.

Just as the ballerina makes leaping gracefully through the air seem effortless and the golfer drives a ball 350 metres with what looks like barely a touch, don't be tricked into thinking that those who deliver with precision, clarity and poise do so without a depth of preparation, dedication and discipline.

Sitting on the couch, listening with muted horror as Cassandra unveiled her plan for us to run the Marathon de Paris in a little over six months, all these thoughts were running through my head, which if you boiled them down had the same two sources as people's fear of speaking in public: (1) A complete lack of *confidence*. I had never run anything like a marathon before. My last running experience hadn't been that great and didn't instil in me much confidence going forward. (2) At the same time, a total lack of *clarity*. How do you even prepare to run a marathon? Do you just go out and start running and hope for the best?

So I called my dad. The fact that he had completed at least one more marathon than I had made him my obvious go-to expert on the subject.

'Dad, Cass and I have decided to run the marathon with you next year, but I have no idea where to start the preparation.' He reassured me that if we were willing to do the work it was quite possible for us to run the marathon in six months. I should make it clear that I wasn't training to win, just to finish (ahead of my wife).

The next day Dad sent me an email with a running plan attached. It wasn't like any running plan I had seen before. It had a column of dates, counting down to the marathon, and a column of times. That was it.

I was confused. Where were the distances? How far was I supposed to run? I thought he might have sent me the wrong file, so I called him up to ask what was going on.

'All I want you to do is follow the process and get out on the road and start running,' was his response. 'Fifteen minutes today, twenty minutes tomorrow and so on.' It didn't make much sense to me. It wasn't what I was used to, but once I got out on the road and followed the plan, I soon found I was actually getting better at it.

It was the intersection of *process* and *practice*.

When I work with clients in my practice, I tell them that their two main hurdles – lack of *confidence* and lack of *clarity* – can best be addressed by *practice* and *process*.

For lack of *confidence*... *practice*. You get better when you're out on the road running. You get better at speaking in public when you get out there and do it. Volunteer to speak at conferences, town halls and team meetings. Give speeches at weddings, birthdays and funerals. Every time you speak, you learn and grow.

For lack of *clarity*... *process*. You'll find a lot more clarity when you have a process to follow. Something to show you where to start, where to go and what to do. It doesn't need to be the process in this book (although I have no doubt you'll find it valuable), but find something that works for you. Treat it like scaffolding around your opportunity to speak, or training wheels on a bike. Keep using it until you feel confident to ride without it.

In *Lead the Room* you're going find the balance between *process* and *practice*. I'm going to explore concepts and ideas that will give you a *process*. But the *practice* decision is up to you. The opportunity to get out on the road and start running using these concepts is a decision you're going to need to make for yourself.

Six months after that first conversation about running the marathon we were in Paris standing at the starting line alongside more than 50,000 other runners from around the world. The energy was palpable, and the crowd let out a huge cheer as the race began. At the 35-kilometre mark I glanced at Cassandra and mumbled words to the effect of, 'If you've still got any energy left in the tank feel free to run on ahead – no need to wait for me', thinking in my head she would stay with me. She did not.

After more than five hours of nonstop running through the Parisian streets and parks I approached the finish line to see Cassandra and my father standing there waiting and cheering me on. It was an emotional moment when I crossed the line and completed a goal I had so recently thought impossible.

It wasn't that I was anything special. I wasn't a natural-born athlete. But I had decided to follow the process and do the work, getting out there and putting in the practice.

That's something anyone can do. Including you.

INTRODUCTION

DON'T JUST SPEAK. LEAD.

You don't need another book on presentation skills. I get that, and that's not really what I'm here for. My goal in writing this book isn't to help you become a better speaker. I want to help you become a more effective leader. I'm happy if this book helps you nail your next presentation, but I'd much rather equip you to leverage your platform to lead and mobilise your team. In the process of helping you do that, I hope you will become better at public speaking too.

When people hear the words 'public speaking', their thoughts tend to race in all kinds of directions. Usually starting with something like 'I hate public speaking' or 'I really need to get better at that'. Then the questions start rolling in:

How do I get better?
How do I project my voice more?
How do I structure a presentation?
How long should I speak for?
How do I deal with nerves?
How can I influence decision-makers?
How much should I practise?
How do I tell great stories?

All of these are valuable questions, some of which I may even address in this book. But do you notice something that all of them have in common? It's that first word.

How.

We want to know the tips and tricks, the tactics and tools to help us become more confident communicators and leaders. We want the shortcuts to success because, let's face it, we are pretty impatient.

Can you name this painting? And the artist? Would you visit a museum to see it? Probably not.

The danger in looking for quick-fix solutions is we often miss the bigger picture. Zoom out and you get the context of what you are looking at.

My goal is to do the same for your leadership and the way you communicate. To think bigger than the idea of presentation skills training. To think holistically about how you can communicate and connect more effectively to build and leverage your leadership platform to lead at scale. This is less about public speaking than about *platform leadership*.

When people ask *how*, I often find they are looking at a small part of a much bigger picture. And in my opinion it's one of the least important parts.

A few years ago, I was attending a conference in Melbourne where I had spent some time working with a couple of the people presenting. I decided to sit in on one of the other sessions. There was a speaker who was generating some great buzz around the conference hallways and I wanted to hear what all the hype was about.

The MC introduced the speaker, who made her way on stage and began to share her journey. It was an extremely powerful story of overcoming obstacles and personal resilience. I try not to overanalyse keynote presentations, but I couldn't help but pick up on a few things. Mostly that she was *doing everything wrong...* technically. She was reading heavily from notes, dropped in a few cuss words, didn't have a lot of stage presence, didn't hold her hands the right way or have dazzling PowerPoint slides. And yet everyone in the room was hanging on her every word. When the presentation finished people gave her a standing ovation and waited in line to speak with her until she had to leave.

Contrast this with another speaker I watched recently, who did everything as though he had written the book on presentation skills. He had the hand gestures, the slides, the projection and the humour down pat. He didn't need notes and he showed just the right amount of vulnerability. Yet I looked around the room and people didn't seem to connect in the same way; they applauded politely and moved on. It was like he was getting everything right and wrong at the same time.

Why? There is so much more to *leading a room* than being a great speaker or delivering a polished presentation. When people ask a question that begins with *how*, I often tell them they are missing two-thirds of a much bigger picture (see Figure 1).

Figure 1: The Lead the Room model

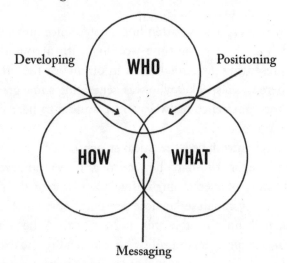

Who – *who you are*

I have learned that it's not just what you do but also who you are that is important. When people hear your name, what do they think and feel? What kind of reputation have you built? Do they find you credible? What have you done that has helped position you as someone they think is worth listening to? When you stand up to speak, do you feel comfortable in your own skin or are you busy comparing yourself with other people in the room? Are people seeing the real you? Who are you when no-one is watching?

What – *what you say*

There's a difference between saying something and having something valuable to say. When you stand up to speak, have you taken time to understand the value of what you are saying to your audience and not just to you? Do you have a clear, memorable and succinct message to communicate? Do you know how to deliver that message in a way that cuts through to and connects with the people you are speaking to?

How – *how you say it*

Do you know how to get better at delivering your message in a way that connects? Are you learning, growing and improving? Are you using the tools available to you to get your message across better? Are you dealing with the anxiety of speaking in public and getting feedback from others to help you improve?

If you want to *lead the room*, you need to think much more broadly than just *how* you deliver a presentation.

Imagine this. You're sitting at home and there's a knock on your front door. You weren't expecting visitors. You open the door and standing before you is a person you've never met with a set of keys in their hand.

'Hi there, sorry to interrupt you. But would you mind getting in my car so we can go for a drive.'

You'd have to be a pretty trusting person to say yes. If you're like me, your response is going to be, 'It's not happening, buddy'.

'But I'm a really good driver. I've been driving for over 20 years. I even know how to parallel park.'

The parallel parking thing is impressive, but that's not enough to get me into the car. It just isn't enough that you know *how* to drive. I'm asking much bigger questions: 'Who are you?' and 'Why?'

Communication is an incredibly powerful vehicle for change. It helps move people from where they are to where we need them to be. It's like having a giant bus to get your employees where you need them to go, not only faster but a whole lot easier. But if we want to get them on the bus, they need to trust the driver (you), they need a compelling reason to get in the car (your message) and they'll want the experience to be enjoyable (your delivery).

I have some friends who are not the best drivers. For privacy reasons I won't say who they are, although I'm very tempted to name and shame. That said, it doesn't mean I avoid them. I'm usually just a little cautious about getting in the car with them. You don't need to be a master presenter for people to follow you or to be an influential leader, but it does help to create a much smoother journey.

MOMENTS THAT MATTER

In the moments that really matter, leadership really matters.

Ask anyone old enough to remember September 11, 2001, and it's likely they will be able to recount in vivid detail exactly where they were and what they were doing on the morning news broke of a cruel, coordinated and catastrophic terrorist attack on the United States involving four passenger airliners. The attack, which killed nearly 3,000 people and injured over 6,000 more, changed the security landscape of air travel and remains a painful moment etched into human history.

While people around the globe sat together glued to their television sets, attempting to process and make sense of the unspeakable tragedy unfolding before their eyes, news outlets and journalists were working overtime to keep up with the breaking news. And yet, with the wealth of information available to viewers on every channel, newspaper and online outlet, people across the United States and the world were not just waiting for someone to *inform* them. In that moment, they were looking for someone to stand up and *lead* them.

That night President George W. Bush faced the television cameras and delivered what would become a history-making Presidential Address to the Nation and the world. Irrespective of your political views (and many would criticise him during his two terms), few would argue that this speech and these words were what America needed most in that moment.

> *'A great people has been moved to defend a great nation. Terrorist attacks can shake the foundations of our biggest buildings, but they cannot touch the foundation of America. These acts shatter steel, but they cannot dent the steel of American resolve. America was targeted for attack because we're the brightest beacon for freedom and opportunity in the world. And no-one will keep that light from shining.'*

In your own leadership journey you are unlikely to be required to deliver an address of such weight and gravity, but you will face opportunities to communicate and lead in moments that matter to you and your organisation. Whether in a television interview or online video, a town hall or your weekly stand-up meeting, the nature of leadership means you will find yourself standing in front of a group of people at a moment that demands you do more than just speak – it compels you to *lead*.

Every opportunity to speak is a moment either to build or to burn your leadership platform. James C. Humes, speech-writer for five American Presidents, said it this way:

> *'The art of communication is the language of leadership. Every time you speak, you are auditioning for leadership.'*

Take a moment to think about the last presentation you gave or the last opportunity you had to communicate an important message to your team. How did it position you as a leader in the organisation? Did you use the opportunity to leverage your leadership platform?

What about the opportunity to speak that you thought was better delegated to someone else? How did *not* speaking in that moment limit your potential and rob you of the opportunity to lead from your platform?

When it comes to leading an organisation, every leader fundamentally understands the consequences of a poor leadership approach to finances. We understand the consequences of a poor leadership approach to processes or change management. But how many leaders are fully aware of the consequences of a poor leadership approach to communication?

The impact of ineffective or non-existent communication is felt throughout the organisation. It shows up in higher turnover, absenteeism, negativity and stress; and it perpetuates lower engagement, morale, innovation and productivity. A report from SIS International Research in partnership with Siemens Communications found that an organisation with as few as 100 employees could be leaking over half a million dollars every year as a result of communications barriers and latency.

In a 2013 article, Glassdoor for Employers listed the top five reasons 'Why Employees Love Their CEOs'. It wasn't surprising to read that employees want a leader who is visible both inside and outside the company. Seeing their leader leveraging their platform externally increased pride felt by employees. Hearing regularly from their leader internally, whether they are walking the corridors, writing notes or holding regular town hall meetings, created a culture of accessibility and boosted morale.

There are no unimportant moments to speak, because every moment you stand in front of your team or organisation is an opportunity to lead. It's an opportunity to leverage your platform to accomplish collectively in a moment something that might have taken weeks or months to accomplish individually.

Think about some of these examples of *moments that matter*. Whether you're ready for them or not, as a leader you'll need to know how to communicate effectively and lead your way through them. You'll need to be ready to communicate a message that counts.

Moments of pioneering – *implementing change*

It has been said that *change is the only constant*. As a leader you can be certain that you will be required to help guide your team through complex change and transition. Some of that change will take you into unfamiliar territory as you pioneer in new spaces. You will need to paint a picture of your desired future, while at the same time intentionally shift fixed mindsets and dysfunctional thinking that causes people to stay where they are.

Moments of sensemaking – *creating clarity*

You will experience moments of uncertainty when the narrative is open to interpretation. It is in these moments that leaders distinguish themselves. If you cannot tell the story, your people – or worse, someone else – will do it for you. Great leaders view people and circumstances differently and need to help others do the same. You will be required to make sense of uncertainty and chaos and to control the narrative through clearly articulated and compelling messaging.

Moments of confronting or reinforcing – *shaping culture*

Every time you speak is an opportunity to reinforce and shape your desired culture. By culture, I don't just mean what you want people to do but who you want people to be. The stories you share, the behaviour you confront and the behaviour you reward paint a picture of your culture and reinforce the way things get done here.

Moments of bonding – *building connection*

Every moment you have to speak is an opportunity to build and strengthen trust and connection with your team, and trust is a foundation for growth. John Maxwell writes, 'Teams that don't bond, can't build'.

Moments of mobilising – *casting a compelling vision*

Do you have a compelling vision or a common purpose to rally around and move towards? Do you know how to communicate it? In his book *Amplifiers*, Matt Church writes, 'It's been said that when Caesar spoke men wept, but when Cicero spoke men marched'. For a leader, to inspire people is valuable but to mobilise people towards action is better.

Moments of influencing – *strengthening commitment*

Do you have great ideas? Do you want people to buy into those ideas? Do you need something from people? The ability to influence people by articulating and communicating the value of your ideas is a critical leadership skill.

Moments of steering – *navigating crisis*

There is a challenge and then there is a crisis. As a leader you will be required to navigate both. Like an airline pilot, you will be the calm voice of authority coming over the intercom while steering the organisation through turbulent weather. You will be the steady adviser and voice of reason in seemingly unreasonable circumstances.

Moments of translating – *managing complexity*

Can you apply your high-level strategy in low-level situations? Can you turn your ideas into strategy and communicate that strategy to generate action? Can you articulate complex information in a jargon-free way that is useful for your team and organisation? In moments that matter, you need to be able to communicate a message that counts. It's the difference between a person who speaks and a leader who leads.

In 1997, Apple was on the ropes. According to an article in *The New York Times*, 'The Silicon Valley pioneer was being decimated by Microsoft and its many partners in the personal-computer market. It had just cut a third of its work force, and it was about 90 days from going broke.'

Steve Jobs, when he returned to Apple 12 years after being forced out, faced a *moment that mattered*. His team had gathered for an internal staff meeting that in hindsight would become a pivotal call to arms for the staff at Apple. Look up this staff meeting on YouTube and you can hear the language of his presentation. This wasn't just any internal meeting. It was a compelling moment when Jobs stepped out in front of the crowd and pointed to a desired future: a return to the core values of Apple. It was a quest for the organisation and its team to become truly great again.

> *'We've got some incredibly exciting product announcements coming up soon. Some incredibly exciting things in general are going to be happening over the next 90 to 120 days. And I really deeply appreciate all of the commitment that's in this room and with the people not in this room for turning this company around. This company is absolutely going to turn around. As a matter of fact, I think the question now is not "Can we turn Apple around?" I think that's the booby prize. I think it's "Can we make Apple really great again?"'*

I'm not suggesting it was this meeting alone that transformed Apple into becoming the first trillion-dollar US publicly listed organisation, but it does give a glimpse behind the curtain to a leader who wasn't afraid to step out front and be visible in the important moments; a leader people would get behind and follow to the promised land that awaited them.

Will you be that kind of leader? What kind of leader do you want to be?

WHAT KIND OF LEADER DO YOU WANT TO BE?

A couple of years after completing my undergraduate marketing degree I found myself back on campus. No longer a student, this time I was employed in the division of marketing focusing on student recruitment. It was a full-circle moment and an exciting time to be part of the team as we navigated a significant rebranding exercise and launched the university's most coordinated marketing campaign ever.

The campaign centred on the message 'Be What You Want to Be'. The university wanted to highlight graduate outcomes and success stories, and to show prospective students that if they chose the pathway through tertiary education, they could find themselves in the place they most wanted to be. In essence, we said, if you're ready to do the work you *can* be what you want to be.

What kind of leader do you want to be? What is the pathway that will help you be that leader, and are you ready to do the work to get you there? If you are, then this book is for you.

Working with leaders and teams across Australia, I have found that most leaders want to influence those they lead in a positive way. They want to make a difference. They want to lead and mobilise their team around a common purpose or vision.

Unfortunately, many don't realise that their current pathway or actions won't get them to that place.

In my practice, I'm passionate about helping leaders find a pathway that will help them get where they want to be. It starts by being honest with where they are right now.

Imagine this pathway as a ladder to becoming the leader you want to be (see Figure 2). Where are you on this ladder right now? What kind of leader are you?

Avoid

The Invisible Leader – people disconnect

If you're this leader, chances are you feel sick at the very thought of standing up to speak in front of a group of people. Maybe you've done it before and had a negative experience or watched someone else have a negative experience. Your confidence may have taken a hit or two. If it isn't a lack of confidence, maybe it's just not a priority for you right now. You have plenty on at the moment, and the last thing you have time for is preparing to speak at a town hall. Why not just pass this one on to your HR or Comms leader? That's their role, right?

What I commonly hear when I speak with teams is that they feel *disconnected* from this kind of leader. They say things like:

> *'I never hear from him.'*
> *'I don't even know what we are working towards.'*
> *'She doesn't communicate.'*
> *'There's no vision or direction here.'*

This often shows up in staff engagement surveys as low scores in 'communication', and that's a fair criticism. As I often tell the leaders I work with, you can't follow an invisible leader. If you aren't visible, then you can't be leading.

Figure 2: Platform leadership ladder

		FOCUS	RESULT	EFFORT:IMPACT
		THE RESPECTED LEADER		
BUILDING PLATFORM		**INFLUENCE**	People *Change*	**1:10**
		CONNECT	People *Trust*	**1:6**
		COMMUNICATE	People *Engage*	**1:3**
BURNING PLATFORM		**SPEAK**	People *Listen*	**1:1**
		RESIST	People *Disengage*	**8:1**
		AVOID	People *Disconnect*	**10:1**
		THE INVISIBLE LEADER		

Resist

The Indifferent Leader – people disengage

The indifferent leader doesn't want to be there any more than the people they're speaking to. You can see it in their eyes that they don't want to be doing this and can't wait for it to be over. They'll say yes, but then look for every opportunity to get out of it if they can. They likely don't think a lot about investing in the skills to improve their communication because it's not something they want to do more of.

What I commonly hear from their teams is that they feel *disengaged* every time their leader speaks. I hear them say things like:

'Our leader is boring.'
'I have no idea why he spoke or what he was talking about.'
'She never prepares for opportunities to speak.'

When I talk to these leaders, they blame the audience:

'Every time I speak, their eyes glaze over; they don't focus.'
'I say the same things over and over and nothing seems to stick.'
'These people just aren't getting it.'

Every time you speak and people find themselves disengaging you reinforce your reputation, making it increasingly difficult to engage people when you speak on future occasions.

Speak

The Typical Leader – *people listen*

Most people I work with locate themselves at this stage of the pathway. It's like being in neutral: there's a lot of noise but no movement. It's the mindset that says, 'I'll speak, you listen'. They tend to be less concerned about whether people are getting what is being said and more concerned about making sure they get out everything they want to say. They usually aren't any more confident than the people lower down the ladder, but they deal with the occasion as they would rip off a bandaid: grin and bear it and hope it's over quickly.

When I talk to their teams, I hear things like:

'I felt like I was being talked at rather than communicated with.'
'It was just a big information/brain dump on us.'

'There was a lot covered, but we don't actually know what we're supposed to do with it.'

Operating as this kind of leader isn't going to kill your career, but neither will it set you on a forward path to leading and mobilising people. You're not going to be the kind of leader people line up behind and say, 'We're with you, let's go'.

Communicate

The Inspiring Leader – *people engage*

When I work with leaders and teams my goal is to shift them to a place where they operate above the line of limiting potential, a place where they learn how to communicate in such a way that people want to engage with them. When they speak, the way they deliver a message ensures that people not only show up; they switch on to what is being said. You can see the lights go on around the room. You watch as people lean forward in their seats in anticipation for what comes next. It's a room where people put their phones away and start to hang on the words you're sharing. It's the kind of communication that engages and inspires teams. It feels more like a dialogue than a monologue, because people aren't just listening to you – they become part of the conversation.

Connect

The Credible Leader – *people trust*

Imagine, as you stand up to speak, feeling the weight of support from people in the room. What would it feel like if you knew that the people you were speaking to were with you and trusted you? Effective communication breaks down the barriers to trust. As in any great relationship, trust is foundational to building a strong team. It is the currency of organisational commitment. People don't just want to go somewhere; they want to go *with* someone they trust.

Influence

The Respected Leader – *people change*

The goal of every great leader is to be deeply respected by those they lead. Only then will their words have weight and result in real progress and change. These are the leaders who don't just share an idea; they mobilise people around a cause. When they stand up to speak, people listen with respect and gratitude. They don't just take on board what has been said; they carry those words and apply them to see change happen and momentum build.

Throughout this book my goal is to help you move up this pathway to become the leader you want to be, the leader who operates above the limitation line, who leverages their potential and builds their leadership platform. I want you to become the respected leader who makes a difference to those you lead, to connect and build trust and engage those you speak to.

THE THREE BIG OBSESSIONS

In the three parts of this book we are going to explore what I teach my clients as the 'Three Big Obsessions of Great Communicators', which lie at the intersections of these three ideas.

1. *Positioning* – the intersection of WHO you are and WHAT you say
2. *Messaging* – the intersection of WHAT you say and HOW you say it
3. *Developing* – the intersection of HOW you say it and WHO you are.

These obsessions are treated separately here, but that doesn't at all mean they are separate. You don't progress sequentially from Positioning to Messaging to Developing, nor do you ever really 'arrive', so to speak. The goal is progress, not perfection. As a leader, when you deliver your messaging you are simultaneously thinking about your positioning. As you deliver your messaging you are also thinking about how you can be developing. None of these activities holds greater weight than the others; each is important and potent.

When writing this I hesitated for a moment about using the word *obsession*. It is a strong word to use and I didn't want to give the impression of this as the aggressive pursuit of perfection, because that isn't the case. When I think of an obsession, I think of the way you might fall in love with an idea. The way that idea is always rolling around in your head and you can't help but think about it. Like an entrepreneur starting a new business or two people falling in love, you can't seem to get the idea out of your head. That's my vision with these three obsessions. You fall in love with the ideas and think about them all the time. When you're preparing to speak, you think about them. When you're having a conversation with a colleague, they sit in the back of your mind. When you get feedback that is designed to help you grow, you think about them.

So let's get started.

PART 1
POSITIONING

Great communicators obsess about *positioning*. While a great presentation might demonstrate to people *what* you know, positioning is ultimately about how you become *known*. The word 'position' comes from the Latin word *ponere*, which means to place. I think about positioning as how people place you in their mind.

One of my favourite questions to ask a new group of people I am training or an individual I am mentoring is:

What is one positive word people in your team or organisation might use to describe you and your leadership?

It's a question I was asked when gaining my Gallup Strengths Certification, and it's designed to help you start a conversation around strengths-based development. But when I thought more deeply on this question, I realised there is so much more insight you can get from how people respond.

Take a moment to think about it for yourself. What word would you use?

If you're struggling to think of a response, you aren't alone. Most often when I ask this question I'm met with nervous laughter. There is of course always the one entertainer in the room who boldly declares, 'I couldn't think of just one'. But the bigger and more important question here is:

Is this how you want to be known?

If you could choose how people talked about you, what would you want them to say? If you could create an image in the minds of your audience or your followers that informed their thinking, what would it be?

Well, you can. That's what positioning is all about. Taking time to understand deeply who you are and what you know, then making a conscious and intentional effort to communicate that to people in what you say and do.

One of my favourite examples of the impact of intentional positioning is the 'We Try Harder' campaign for Avis Car Hire. It was a tagline they adopted in the early sixties and kept for 50 years until a change in 2012. I remember first learning about it when studying for my undergraduate degree in marketing and being fascinated by their approach to what could have been thought as a setback. As a company that was stuck in the number two position behind Hertz, they were asked by new advertising agency Doyle Dane Bernbach, 'Why do people hire from you?' They wanted to know what it was that made Avis the company it was. The response they elicited was simple: 'We Try Harder.' When you're positioned in the number two place you have to work harder. This was a light-bulb moment for them. From that point on their positioning focus shifted away from trying to be number one to being known for their outstanding customer service. Not only was it effective in building their brand reputation, but it also took the company from a loss of $3.2 million to a profit, for the first time in 13 years, of $1.2 million.

Positioning is the key to getting people on the bus with you, because ultimately people want to know *who* they are getting on the bus with. Knowing how to drive or having a great destination is important, but most likely meaningless if you are unable to get people to go with you. I have found that people don't just want to *go somewhere*, they also want to go *with someone*.

With the rise in the marketplace of a digital native generation who spend more time looking at the world through a screen, the concept of *personal branding* is at the forefront of the conversation. Branding is no longer just a conversation for the corporate marketing department, and anonymity is fast becoming a luxury of the past. Our lives are on display and people are always watching. But positioning is more than just building your own personal brand. It runs much deeper and broader than that.

In Part 1 we will explore four positioning activities that every leader can actively engage in:

1. *Developing your character* – who you really are

2. *Leading your narrative* – what you say you are

3. *Building your credibility* – who people see you are

4. *Managing your reputation* – what people hear you are.

As you read this part of the book you may find yourself wondering, *How am I supposed to be thinking about this every time I get up to speak?* That is understandable. What you are about to read is designed to help expand your thinking about how you carry yourself as a leader on a daily basis, not just when you have to speak. To do this requires investment over time. As you read, take notes of what stands out that you need to work on and start there. Come back and read this regularly and build on what you have started. Leadership is a long game, not a short sprint to the finish line.

CHAPTER 1
DEVELOP YOUR CHARACTER

The spotlight does not *make* a leader, it *reveals* one.

The spotlight that highlights your best features is often the same one that exposes your worst. As a leader you can *tell* people as much as you like, 'This is who I am', but eventually it is who you *really* are that people will come to see. Developing your character focuses on bringing alignment between your *talk* and your *walk*.

In early 2017, former Uber CEO Travis Kalanick learned the harsh truth of the leadership spotlight when dashcam footage of a heated altercation between him and Uber driver Fawzi Kamel on dropping fare prices was leaked online and gained strong media attention. Kalanick was quick to issue a formal apology to his team that read:

> 'By now I'm sure you've seen the video where I treated an Uber driver disrespectfully. To say that I am ashamed is an extreme understatement. My job as your leader is to lead ... and that starts with behaving in a way that makes us all proud. That is not what I did, and it cannot be explained away. It's clear this video is a reflection of me – and the criticism we've received is

a stark reminder that I must fundamentally change as a leader and grow up.' (news.com.au)

He went on to say that this was the first time he'd been willing to admit that he needed leadership help.

Although he apologised to Fawzi, to the driver and rider community, and to the Uber team, it wasn't enough. The back-wash from this and a number of other events saw the chief executive stand down from his position in June that year. Later, *The Economic Times* in India wrote a piece on Kalanick that explored the affair. What stood out for me when I read the article was the concept of foundations. They wrote:

> *'Kalanick was regarded as the most vocal champion of the value of hustling and even made it into a motto for his company to follow. However, in the need to "always be hustling", Kalanick and his company seemed to have forgotten the importance of laying down strong business foundations.'*

On a recent flight to Italy Cassandra and I stopped over in Dubai. As we were coming in to land, I was looking out the window as I usually do, taking in the view of a new city. Then I saw it: the Burj Khalifa, the tallest building in the world, towering over the physical landscape around it. Obviously, it was hard to miss, but I was also keenly looking out for it. A few years earlier I had taken time to do some research on the build-ing before speaking to a group of leaders on the importance of building character. The Burj Khalifa perfectly illustrates the importance of foundations.

When you start the construction of the world's tallest build-ing you don't start by going high. You start by going deep. The foundations alone consist of more than 45,000 cubic metres of concrete and 192 piles buried 50 metres deep into the ground.

I'm not a builder or an architect but it makes sense that if you want to build something tall, it should first have a foundation capable of supporting it.

I have learned that character is the foundation that supports leadership growth. You will only grow as high as your foundation runs deep. Talent might get you into a position of influence, but it's character that will keep you there.

I don't use Uber's case study to cast a shadow over the reputation of Travis Kalanick or to suggest that he epitomises a lack of character. I use it to demonstrate the importance for leaders to intentionally think about the development of their character. If they want to elevate their level of influence, they must be willing to dig a deep foundation of character. Character is who we really are, and eventually who people will see. Character is always worth developing.

It seems almost unfair that leaders must hold themselves to a higher standard than others, but this is both the burden and the privilege of leadership. What might be acceptable for some is not acceptable for all. Actions that might be considered insignificant if carried out by someone else can be magnified when you are entrusted to a leadership platform.

In one of my earlier roles, mentoring high-school students in leadership, I had a dictum I repeated regularly:

'Don't forget the wagon you're draggin'!'

It's a silly expression but it had a lot of sentiment attached. I told them of when I was a boy, full of energy and life. Our play world was mainly outdoors. We would climb trees, swim on the lakes, hike through the bush and dig holes in the beach. We did whatever we wanted to, because we could. Then we were given a little red wagon to help us carry around our things. Suddenly we had to think about the places we would go; we couldn't just do anything we wanted, because sometimes it would have meant leaving the wagon behind. If we brought it and tried to do everything we used to, we would end up damaging it. When you're leading, people are following, and you can't just do anything without thought for those behind you. If you do whatever you want, you'll leave people behind; if you try to drag them with you, you may just end up hurting them more than you help them.

It might seem strange to be talking about character and leadership foundations in a book focused on communication, but it's actually an often-overlooked element of effective communication. Every time you speak, there you are. You cannot separate who you are from what you say and do, so you had better make sure you take the time to invest in who you want to be. Stephen R. Covey put it this way: 'You can't talk your way out of a problem you behaved your way into!'

I think there are three commitments you will need to make if you want to build and maintain healthy character. These are lessons I have learned and continue to learn. Like lifting weights at the gym, they are muscles that need to be exercised regularly and consistently.

CREATE HEALTH

What is *in you* will eventually come *out of you*.

For the past few years Cassandra and I have added the word *health* to our vision board. Yes, it includes losing a few kilos, but for us it is so much more than that. What we really want is a holistic kind of health of body and mind. Physical health is no good to us if we aren't mentally healthy. Our health impacts our life. It shapes the way we interact with the people in our world. It changes our motivation and desire to do what we are passionate about, and it affects how we lead and communicate. What I have discovered is that much of our health is built behind the *'seens'*.

Don't mistake what is *unseen* for what is *unimportant*.

Recently I boarded a plane to Sydney on my way to work with a great group of leaders from one of Australia's leading charities. As I sat waiting for the plane to push back I began to think about all the things that were taking place *behind the seens* to get me off the ground – baggage handling, pre-flight briefings, cabin checks, safety checklists, catering and cleaning to name a few.

From where I was seated I couldn't see the pilots, of course, though I'm pretty sure they were up there, or how ever would I get to Sydney? It's clear that just because something is *unseen* it doesn't mean it's *unimportant*.

There was a mango tree not far from the house where I grew up in Queensland. For years any growth in that tree was hidden beneath the soil. It looked like nothing was happening, but all the time it was working away quietly and invisibly, sending roots down deep, building its base, preparing for the future. Finally it broke through the ground and became visible for the first time. Very quickly there was lots of growth and change, but to our disappointment there was no sign of mangoes.

Slowly the tree matured until the day came when it was covered in fruit, ripe and ready to pick. At last the tree was fulfilling the promise for which it had been planted. That day we enjoyed the product of a long, complex and unseen process.

You cannot expect fruit from a tree that hasn't reached maturation, whose branches aren't yet strong enough to carry or sustain it.

Leadership, too, is a ground-up process (see Figure 3), from:

- ROOTS to BRANCHES to FRUIT
- HIDDEN to VISIBLE to HELPFUL
- HEALTH to GROWTH to RESULTS.

Figure 3: Ground-up leadership

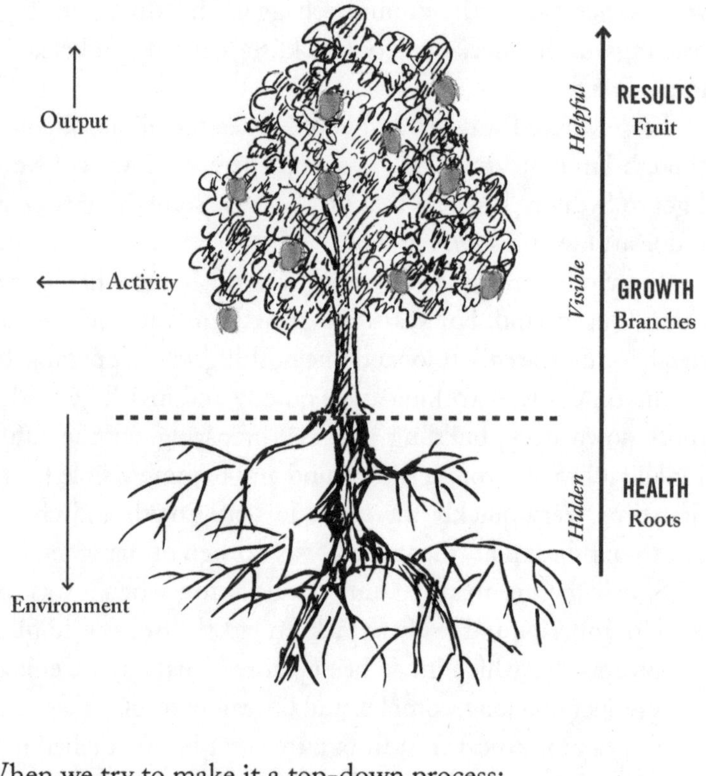

When we try to make it a top-down process:

- We focus on driving outcomes and achieving RESULTS. We demand GROWTH but end up having to deal with issues of poor HEALTH.

- We focus on the FRUIT, making demands of the BRANCHES but neglecting the ROOTS.

But when we build from the ground up:

- We start by creating nurturing environments in which HEALTH is valued. We cultivate GROWTH and development that increases capacity and activity. In return, we achieve outcomes and deliver RESULTS.

- We nurture the ROOTS and GROW the branches, then we enjoy the FRUIT.

Leadership and character are built from the ground up.

When you have a speaking engagement, don't get frustrated with preparation work; it's about getting the roots strong. If you're waiting on a leadership opportunity, find great soil and build your foundations to sustain the journey ahead. If you lead a team, make health a priority and results will follow. If you've got branches that can't produce or sustain fruit, invest in activities that will help them grow and develop.

Creating health is all about building and nurturing the foundations of your leadership. If you know you aren't in a healthy place, your communication will reflect that. What's unseen inside you will eventually be seen in what comes out of you.

STAY HUMBLE

Pride is the enemy of humility.

It's important to understand that humility is not self-deprecation or self-sabotage. I have found myself in many conversations with people who believe that humility is all about deflecting any accolade, attention or affirmation. They are the hardest people in the world to compliment. That's not humble, it's annoying. Rather than a lack of pride, it often signifies a lack of confidence. True humility, as Rick Warren once said, isn't thinking less of yourself but thinking of yourself less.

In *The Trusted Advisor*, Robert M. Galford and his co-authors outline an equation for building trust with four variables. Credibility, reliability and intimacy are in the numerator of the fraction and self-orientation, the fourth variable, is in the denominator. If you want to increase trust, they suggest, then increase the numerator variables; if you want to decrease trust, then increase the denominator. Increase your self-orientation and people will trust you less.

What is self-orientation? It's thinking about ourselves first, making everything about ourselves. You've probably met someone like that. They ask, 'What did you do on the weekend?', then quickly interrupt your reply to tell a story about what *they* did. I've been in conversations with people who practically turn blue holding their breath as they wait for their moment to interject.

When Andy Stanley, a pastor from Atlanta, Georgia, was interviewed on Don Miller's StoryBrand podcast, he spoke of his experience giving a sermon at the pre-inauguration church service for President Obama in 2013 – no pressure! He was given 15 minutes to deliver a message on communication to arguably one of the most influential people in the world at the time. He described it as 'a message to one person with two hundred people watching on'. What would you choose to say? Stanley chose to talk on the thought 'What do you do when you are the most powerful person in the room?' He knew that whatever room the President walked into he would immediately become the most powerful person in that room. His advice to the President: 'You leverage that power for the benefit of other people in the room.' What he was illustrating is that *influence* is used for *service*.

Many of us have been led to believe that humility and confidence exist at opposite ends of the spectrum, that if you are confident you lack humility, and if you accept affirmation without modestly brushing it aside then you are prideful. But it is possible for a leader to be both confident and humble. Pride increases self-orientation. It makes our influence and authority about *us* and strokes our ego. Pride doesn't play nice with vulnerability; after all, why would a proud leader want people to see the messy part of their life? So it prompts you to hide the areas and issues you don't want exposed rather than dealing with them. Out of sight, out of mind, right? Wrong. Better to develop your character and deal with the issues on your own terms than have them exposed through the spotlight of influence.

If you want to develop character, make every effort to stay humble. Not the 'self-deprecating, shying away from influence and total disregard for yourself' type of humble but rather the 'becoming the best version of yourself to be given in service to those you lead' kind of humility.

BUILD BETTER HABITS

It's not just about who you are, but also who you are becoming.

James Clear published his book *Atomic Habits* in October 2018, towards the end of the year when I was beginning to think and dream of the year ahead. Every year I join the multitude who convince themselves that this will be the year they keep their New Year's resolutions. I bought the book because I was determined that this time I would not simply go through the motions of trying and failing. I would build better, stronger and more sustainable habits in my life.

Talking of habits, James writes, 'but fundamentally they are not about *having* something. They are about *becoming*

31

someone'. Rather than just helping us achieve an outcome, our habits are building the type of person we want to become. He goes on to say:

> *'Every action you take is a vote for the type of person you wish to become. No single instance will transform your beliefs, but as the votes build up, so does the evidence of your new identity.'*

If you want to be a leader who is worth listening to and to develop your character, then it goes deeper than single acts of nobility; you need to make a lifelong commitment to building strong personal habits. As Will Durant famously said, 'We are what we repeatedly do. Excellence, then, is not an act, but a habit'.

A mentor of mine, Matt Church, always says, 'You lead best when the best version of me talks to the best version of you'. Habits are all about developing patterns of behaviour that create the best version of us. When we don't take time to prioritise the right habits, we are on a quick path to burnout.

As a leader I always know when the habits of my life aren't helping me become the kind of person I want to be, and they always impact my ability to communicate effectively. No leader sets out to achieve burnout. I can't imagine anyone in a leadership role waking up and thinking, *I wonder what I can do to drive myself into the ground today.*

Marathon runners don't leap straight off the starting line into a sprint in the hope that they'll at least make it to the 25 km mark. They prepare, train and visualise themselves crossing the finish line. They aren't just there to start; they are there to finish. Longevity is every leader's goal.

Leadership is both a privilege and a burden. It is an incredible *opportunity* that demands great *responsibility*. But life is unpredictable. Leaders aren't afforded the luxury of setting aside their leadership role every time life throws a curveball. Much like a ship's captain, we must navigate the ship in all seasons, through calm and turbulent waters.

I haven't always got this right; in fact, at times I've got it very wrong and suffered the consequences. Staying fresh and leading for the long haul takes intentional effort and requires intentional habits. There are four key spaces in which I (along with, I suggest, every leader) need to habitually engage: I liken these to a *bed*, a *table*, a *chair* and a *lamp*.

A bed

We need a space where we can rest.

A good night's sleep is underrated. In his book *Are You Fully Charged?*, Tom Rath unpacks research to suggest that losing just 90 minutes of sleep can reduce daytime alertness by nearly one-third. Put another way, he suggests that missing out on four hours of sleep can produce as much impairment as consuming a six-pack of beer. 'An entire night of sleep loss is equivalent to a blood alcohol level of 0.19.' Yet sleep is often one of the first things a leader will sacrifice.

Less sleep does not mean more productivity. A bed is not just about sleep, but about rest and relaxation too. Rest is not a dirty word for high-calibre leaders; it is critical to their long-term success.

A table

We need a space in which to connect.

It's lonely at the top, they say, but it doesn't have to be. Leadership longevity isn't found in isolation. In an article titled 'Burnout at Work Isn't Just About Exhaustion, It's Also About Loneliness', Emma Seppala and Marissa King suggest 'there is a significant correlation between feeling lonely and work exhaustion'. Operating from a place of loneliness and isolation can have devastating consequences for a leader and for their organisation.

A table, for me, symbolises connection. It is a place where we share meals with friends and family, play board games, celebrate and engage in authentic conversation.

We all need a space like this where we can connect. It may look like regular dinner with friends and family or communing with other members of a professional network. Whatever it looks like for you, don't do your leadership journey alone.

A chair

We need a space in which to think, grow and learn.

When was the last time you were alone with your thoughts? When did you last set aside the time to think through an idea or a new concept?

A Harvard Business School study undertaken in the UK found that commuters who used their travel time to think about and plan their day were happier, more productive and less burned out than people who didn't. Do you have a regular space where you can be alone and intentional with your thoughts?

Whether it's a train seat, a park bench or a comfortable couch at home, a chair represents a place to think, reflect, grow and learn. Being intentional with time to think, process and reflect is extremely valuable.

A lamp

We need a space in which to do things that light us up.

A lamp symbolises light and creative energy. What fills your emotional and energy bucket? What piques your interest, sparks your creativity and fills you with ideas? What causes you to lose yourself in the moment and forget about time?

When was the last time you did that?

Everyone is different. So what lights me up will look different to what does it for you. Here one of the biggest obstacles leaders need to overcome is the guilt of feeling like you 'should be doing something else more important'. The implication is that investing in your own self-care is not valuable, which could not be further from the truth.

Now take a minute to reflect on these spaces. How often do you engage in each of them? What needs to change?

If you feel like you've been taken out at the 25 km mark of your race, you haven't been eliminated or disqualified from the race. It's okay to get back in and start running again. Treat your wounds, take it slow and find your rhythm again. Leadership is a long game.

Think about the regular habits that you engage in. Are they helping you become the person and leader you want to be? Are they developing your character and helping you become the best version of yourself? If not, then it's time to make a change, because who you really are is eventually who people will see.

The word 'character' comes from the Greek word for a *stamping tool*, which evolved to mean 'distinguishing qualities'. I like the picture that a stamping tool creates in my mind. I imagine each decision I make stamping my life with the distinguishing qualities I will become known for. What are you stamping your life with?

Who you are matters. If you want people to listen to you and, more importantly, to follow you, then it starts with being a person who is worth following. Commit to developing your character. Create a healthier you and position yourself for growth. Stay humble and use your influence for service. And build strong habits to become the best version of you.

CHAPTER 2
LEAD YOUR NARRATIVE

Positioning isn't about projecting someone you're not; it's about *intentionally* being who you are. American singer and songwriter Dolly Parton said it this way: 'Figure out who you are. Then do it on purpose.'

At some point every leader must ask themselves a simple question: *How do I want to be known?*

Occasionally when I arrive to pick up my wife from work in the afternoon, I cross paths with her friend Julie. I always know how she will greet my arrival. She'll say something to the effect of 'Hey, Know-Grow!' or 'It's Know-Grow!' Anyone else around would have no idea what's going on, but it always makes me laugh. She calls me Know-Grow because my wife once sent her an article I'd written titled 'The Know Grow Zone'. It was built on the simple idea that you can't grow from the things you don't know, so whenever you become aware of something you don't know you should be grateful because it's an opportunity to grow. I'm not sure why this article more than others stuck in her mind. I could probably count the number of conversations we have had on one hand, but she has created a narrative in her head about the kind of person I am: I'm the know-grow guy.

I follow an account on Twitter called @ShowerThoughts. It's a silly but humorous account designed to provoke thinking around mostly unimportant issues. The kinds of things you think about in the shower or when you are bored. But sometimes it has something important to share. One post I saw read:

'A different version of you exists in the minds of everyone who knows you.'

Think about that for a moment. If you're like most people, then your friends will have a version of you, your family will have a slightly different version and that person you just met at a networking event will likely have a different version again. This isn't to say you are living some kind of duplicitous life or that you're being dishonest. It's just that people will likely see more or less of who you are based on your relationship with them and what you are willing to show them. Inside the minds of the people who know you a narrative is being written. The danger is that most leaders don't stop to consider what that narrative is and how they are contributing to it.

Netflix's former chief talent officer Patty McCord puts it like this: 'If your employees aren't informed by you there's a good chance that they will be misinformed by somebody else.' If you aren't taking control and leading the narrative of how you want to be known as a leader, then someone else is likely writing it for you. Or worse, you may even be writing it without knowing it.

As I noted in this parts introduction, in recent years personal branding has become a hot topic of conversation. This concept has helped us wake up to the reality that everything we do contributes to building a narrative of how we become known.

To take control and lead your personal narrative you will need to create a trusted brand, just as any great organisation does.

Here are three things any leader can do to start leading the narrative.

GET CLEAR

Define clearly how you *want* to be known.

Strong positioning starts with personal clarity and deciding how you want to be known. Each is equally important, and difficult.

Recently I filed a trademark with IP Australia. As I was reading up on the steps involved in lodging an application and getting a better understanding of what makes up a trademark, I came across this:

> *'Your trademark, often called a brand, is your identity.*
> *It's the way you show your customers who you are.'*

When it comes to your leadership and the way you communicate, what is your brand? What are your trademarks? In what ways do you show your audience who you are?

Trademarks can be many things, but by taking just a few of the types listed by IP Australia and doing some self-reflection, you could start to build a picture of what yours could potentially look like.

Think about a single word

If you were to describe how you want to be known in just one word, what would that word be? Perhaps it would be:

- authentic
- strong
- empathetic

- honest
- real
- inspiring
- persuasive
- passionate.

We would all like to think we have many of these characteristics, and maybe you do, but if you could choose just one, which would it be? Is there another descriptor not listed that you would identify with? What matters most to you in the way you lead and communicate?

When we find the word that resonates most deeply within us, it shapes and forms a foundation for how we communicate. It gives us a north bearing for how we want to be known and it begins to shape and lead the narrative in the mind of the people we communicate with. This isn't to say this word won't change, because in fact it changes regularly. Think of it more as an evolution over time as you discover more of who you are.

What about a string of words?

Did you struggle to find one word? What if I gave you a few words to build on? What would the tagline of your leadership be? Think of memorable trademarks such as 'Nike – Just Do It' or 'Subway – Eat Fresh'. Would yours be:

- [Your name] – Believes the Best
- [Your name] – Genuinely Cares
- [Your name] – Speaks Well of Others
- [Your name] – Empowers Others
- [Your name] – Inspires Action
- [Your name] – Tells the Truth.

The tagline for your leadership is the way people might describe you in a hallway conversation. When someone hears you are speaking at the next team meeting, what is their initial response? Does it sound something like 'I love when [insert your name] speaks – he/she always [insert your tagline]'?

What image comes to mind?

When I say 'holiday', what image comes into your mind? Perhaps it takes you straight to your favourite holiday destination. Sitting by the pool, cocktail in hand, or out adventuring and exploring in some exotic destination. What image pops into a person's head when your name comes up in conversation? Is it a good image?

- A smiling face
- An open book
- A helping hand
- A safety net
- A lighthouse.

Our interactions with people leave an impression and help create a narrative. The way we lead and communicate can leave an impression of a leader who cares, engages, empowers and uplifts. A negative interaction can taint a reputation or personal brand.

What do people learn when they check out your social media profile, visit your website, receive an email or have a conversation with you? What are your communication or leadership trademarks? Perhaps these reflections have sowed an idea of your ideal trademark. If you're still struggling, the ultimate test is to ask those around you.

I had a friend who used to say, 'if you want to know what people really think about you, call them when you can see them and they haven't seen you. Watch the expression on their face when they see your number'. Amazon's Jeff Bezos once said, 'Your brand is what people say about you when you're not in the room'.

What do people say about you when you're not in the room? Ask someone who is not afraid to give you the truth. Take a minute and ask them these questions:

- How would you describe me in just a word?

- How would you describe me in a few words?

- What picture comes to mind when you think of me as a leader?

Are their answers different from yours or from what you would like them to be? If so, then there is work to be done in leading your narrative.

BE CONSTRUCTIVE

Think intentionally about how your actions or conversations align with how you want to be known.

Every time you speak, lead, write or interact with another human being you have the opportunity to be constructive or destructive. You are either reinforcing the narrative you want or creating dissonance in the mind of the person you are interacting with.

In an initial coaching session with one of my clients we were discussing the results of her CliftonStrengths® assessment. I like to do this with my clients early on in the coaching journey as it is very insightful for me as a coach as well as for them. Besides, who wouldn't want to know what they do best and how they can use those talents to achieve the best outcomes. If you have never experienced this assessment tool, then I highly recommend you take a moment to explore it for yourself. As we worked through the report we got to the theme called Restorative™.

Gallup suggests that 'people strong in the Restorative™ theme are adept at dealing with problems. They are good at figuring out what is wrong and resolving it'.

It is a very valuable quality to possess. People who are restorative are great at dealing with problems. They are energised by figuring out what's broken and how they can fix it. Unfortunately, this can be misunderstood as negativity. People around them will complain, 'He/she is always so negative and points out all the problems for why something won't work'.

When we talked about this some more, my client told me how she understandably didn't want to be known as the negative person on the team. She needed to start leading her narrative. She didn't have to change who she was at the core or become someone she wasn't; she just needed to start being intentional in her interactions with people. Rather than being the person who pointed out problems, she started to create the narrative that she was a *solution finder*. When she could see a problem that others had not yet noticed, and she was tempted to tell people why it couldn't work, she took the time to think about how they might be able to work around the problem. She then came armed with a solution. Her language became more intentional. Rather than saying 'this won't work', she started saying 'this can work if…'.

Thinking more intentionally, and making small adjustments along the way, can make a big difference. Before you post that article, have that conversation, deliver that talk or respond to that email, take time to consider whether this will help construct the type of narrative you want or whether it might do more harm than good. Work on aligning your words and actions to shape how you will be known.

STAY CONSISTENT

Communicate regularly and consistently how you want to be known.

You don't build a great brand overnight, just as you won't create a strong narrative by saying something once. If you want to be known as a positive person, then your communication needs to have a consistently positive intent. That isn't to say you can't deliver negative feedback, but that feedback must have a positive intent. If you want to be known as someone who is transparent, then you will need to communicate openly and at times vulnerably. Not just once, but consistently.

Nike's tagline 'Just Do It' isn't something they said once in a campaign then hoped for the best. It's a consistent message that has been communicated in everything they have done since 1988. It shouldn't be a surprise that so many people recognise it after 30 years of reinforcement. There's a reason Google can modify their logo on special occasions and people still recognise the brand. It's front and centre for millions of people every day on their homepage. It's consistent. Go anywhere in the world and ask across multiple generations and you'll find people who recognise the Coca-Cola logo. This logo has remained almost unchanged since 1887, so it's no wonder it is one of the world's most valuable brands.

Don't underestimate the power of being *consistent*.

Recently I was having a conversation with someone who was beginning to ask some of these questions of herself. When we boiled it down, she wanted to be known as someone who helped others become more *resilient*. Her life was a case study of resilience, so I wasn't surprised when this theme came through. The challenge wasn't determining how she wanted to be known, but finding a way to consistently reinforce that messaging in everything she did as a leader. The key is just to start somewhere. I gave her the challenge of writing and posting regularly on the theme of *resilience* on LinkedIn for 12 months. It doesn't take long for people to start to develop a narrative.

A few years back my father had a change of season and made a bold move to step out of full-time employment and start his own business. We grew up on a stunning five-acre property situated in the middle of a macadamia nut plantation, so his decision to convert our childhood home into a garden wedding and function centre couldn't have been more appropriate. Given my background in marketing, and of course cheap (free) 'family rates', he reached out and asked if I could help set up some of their branding and positioning.

We needed things to move relatively quickly, so we set up the website, designed some brochures and had all the usual business stationery ready to go. When they went live on the website they were bombarded by enquiries. I wasn't surprised, because the setting is absolutely beautiful. There was only one small issue. After spending huge amounts of time quoting and preparing the proposals for each potential customer they would send through the finalised quote, only to be met with a deafening silence. These prospects were never to be heard from again.

This wasn't great news for the new business. Evidently something wasn't right. When we got together to talk we realised there was an issue that revolved around their pricing. It wasn't that they were too expensive, but that there was a disconnect between how they had positioned themselves in the market and how they had priced themselves. There's no question that they are a premier function and wedding venue. But every bit of communication we had built had sent the message that this was just like any other garden venue, and believe me it was not.

We started again, rebuilt the website and redesigned the price list. They added their updated price list to the website to underscore their status as a premier venue. Enquiries dropped off significantly, but this wasn't a bad thing because the ones they received now were from the people who came for the right reasons.

As much as I'd like to say that a simple website and brochure redesign made all the difference, that's not how it works. Consistently and regularly over the past few years they have maintained their positioning as a premier function venue. They have been uncompromising in their standards and in how they communicate, and they are now starting to see the benefits that this positioning has granted them. People come to them for a wedding or function only when they are looking for the best.

I often tell my clients that positioning is a dripping tap, not a firehose. You don't just dump everything and hope for the best. It's not a spray-and-pray approach. It's a process that is clear, constructive and consistent. It's knowing who you are and how you want to be known, thinking intentionally about every action and every word, and communicating that regularly and consistently.

If you want to communicate a message that counts, then start by building a personal brand that people trust. Don't just let your narrative happen. Lead it. Discover who you are then be that person intentionally.

CHAPTER 3
BUILD YOUR CREDIBILITY

Credibility speaks louder than capability.

A few years ago I was attending a leadership conference with Cassandra and a few of our friends. There was a long list of well-known leaders in the line-up of speakers, so it naturally attracted a big crowd. The speakers were a mix of local and international guests, many we had heard of, but a few we hadn't. During one of the sessions we had the opportunity to hear from two very different speakers. One was an international guest who was presenting at the conference for the first time. He was well known in his own country but relatively unheard of here in Australia. The second speaker was a leadership *legend* who has spent nearly four decades investing in and developing leaders all over the globe. Both speakers were brilliant in their own way.

As I sat and listened to the first speaker it was obvious this wasn't his first rodeo. He had everything running like a well-oiled machine, knowing exactly when to pause for laughter and how to work the crowd when they were starting to drift off. Technically speaking, he was a very talented communicator and, all credit to him, he delivered a brilliant idea and made it look easy.

Then the second speaker was introduced – and the room erupted as people surged to their feet. I wondered if the applause would ever stop, and by the look of it so did the speaker, who thanked the audience with great humility once people had regained their seats. A physical shift had taken place in the audience, as people sat up and leaned forward to catch every word. You could feel a current of energy in the room. People tapped 'Record' on their iPhone or took hand-written notes, scribbling frantically to keep up.

If you compared the two speakers, purely from a technical perspective, I would have to say that the first speaker had a much better delivery. Yet it was as if the second speaker had attached giant lead weights to every one of his words. The first speaker was shadow boxing with good form while the second speaker delivered a knockout punch.

I have learned and witnessed how credibility adds 'weight' to your words, and though this quality is intangible, for a leader it is invaluable. Talent is important, but while it might get you a *platform*, it's credibility that will give you a *voice*. John Baldoni put it this way:

> *'Credibility is a leader's coin of the realm. With it, she can lead people to the Promised Land; without it, she wanders in the desert of lost expectations. Once lost it may be impossible to regain, and so the lesson to any manager who has any aspiration of achieving anything is to guard your credibility and take care you never lose it.'*

If you want to deliver a message that counts, if you want to lead and mobilise people, then you need to be willing not just to develop your talent but to build your credibility. Position does not automatically give you *permission* to be heard. Credibility is the key that unlocks the door to permission. If I believe you are credible, I can trust you and will give you permission to speak, and that is a currency worth its weight in gold.

The world of social media is volatile. Those brave souls who dare venture into the world of post comments will understand what I mean. Even the most well-meaning posts can be taken out of context and misconstrued. If you took on board every criticism or comment, you would drive yourself crazy. So it makes sense that we should listen to credible voices rather than just every person who has an opinion. The same is true for your team and audience. Being the boss might make people listen to you, but if you want to be heard you need to build your credibility. You need to give people a *reason* to listen.

And sorry to be the bearer of bad news, but you don't build credibility overnight. Credibility is a long game built over time. What's more, you can spend a lifetime trying to build it and yet break it in a moment. Take a look at the privacy issues surrounding Facebook or the royal commission into banking here in Australia for two examples of the impact that damaged credibility can have both on sentiment and bottom line. The global trust index, produced by the Edelman Trust Barometer, a global study into trust in major institutions, currently languishes at *distruster* level. In 2017–18 the United States experienced the steepest decline in trust ever measured. Today's leaders cannot assume trust and credibility; we must be willing to build it and earn it.

In a *Harvard Business Review (HBR)* article, 'The High Cost of Lost Trust', Tony Simons explores the impact of trust and credibility on business leaders. He articulates it this way:

'The label of "hypocrite" is stickier than its opposite. It takes evidence of only a single lie for a manager to be branded a "liar." In contrast, a person has to tell a whole lot of truth to qualify as a "straight shooter." Credibility, as we have all seen, is slow to build and quick to dissipate. A generally straightforward manager who is caught breaking an important promise will likely have trouble recovering.'

I'm in no way saying that once you lose your credibility you will no longer have any impact or opportunity to lead and mobilise your people. I am saying that once you lose your credibility, you face a long, hard road of intentional work to restore, rebuild and regain it. So it is well worth taking the time to build it, maintain it and guard it with your life.

But how do you build credibility?

Like so many qualities discussed in this book, credibility is a process that takes time and investment. There are five levels (see Figure 4) I have seen leaders move through in building their leadership credibility over time. Moving from one level to the next is not a promotion, nor does your work at the previous level stop happening once you move on; rather, each level is a brick in a wall built over time, with each new course encompassing everything that happens below it.

Figure 4: Five levels of leadership credibility

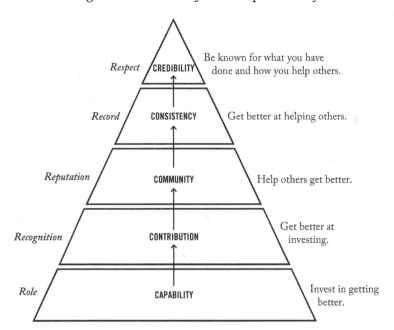

Capability

Invest in getting better.

To an extent people will listen to a technical expert because they know something and are good at what they do. When I have a problem with my car, I don't take just anyone's advice on what I should do to fix it; I take it to a mechanic because that person has a level of credibility. While having technical expertise isn't the pinnacle of credibility, taking time to invest in getting better at what you do or what you know will give you an advantage over those who don't. If you want to speak credibly about something, it stands to reason that you should have some runs on the board.

I was once having dinner with a friend who travels widely as a full-time specialist teacher. I asked him to share one of the biggest lessons he had taken away from his experience. He told me, 'I've learned that if I want to teach people, I need to make sure I'm the smartest person in the room on that topic. It takes a lot of work and commitment, so I'm always looking for opportunities to grow and develop'.

Of course you don't have to be the smartest person in the room to be credible, but you should never stop investing in and getting better at what you know or do.

Contribution

Get better at investing.

As a leader you have valuable skills, expertise and knowledge. How are you sharing it with your organisation and the world? How are you consistently applying and executing your skills and expertise? I have met many brilliant leaders and content experts who are the best-kept secret in their organisation because they don't share what they know or do. You don't win an Australian Open by being the best tennis player in your backyard. People will listen to a leader who they see has some skin in the game. Your team want to know they are following a leader who can achieve results and produce organisational outcomes. They also want to see that you are willing to share and invest what you know.

Are you regularly speaking at team gatherings or town-hall meetings and investing what you know, or do you avoid and delegate those opportunities to other leaders? Are you communicating regularly through your social media channels or staff intranet? Are you volunteering to speak at industry conferences to position yourself within your field of expertise? These may sound like big steps to take, but they are important if you want to build your credibility. You may hate the idea of speaking publicly, but why not just start with an internal meeting. Get better at investing in your people, and as they see the results of your investment you build your permission to speak.

Community

Help others get better.

By sharing and contributing what you know, over time you will build a community of people who follow you for what you know. Eventually you will need to transition from being an *expert* (the best at what you do) to being a *mentor* (helping others become the best). To do so you will need to learn how to set aside your ego and the fear of others succeeding and to invest in the development of others. You will never look worse by helping others get better.

I live in Melbourne, where AFL is king, but my formative years in Queensland have meant that once a year when the State of Origin season arrives I break out my true Maroon colours. I'm not a big sports guy, but something about the State of Origin brings it out in me. For international readers or Victorian residents, State of Origin is a best-of-three rugby league series between the states of Queensland and New South Wales. Or, as many like to refer to it, as New South Wales vs Australia (though perhaps this is the Melbourne vs Sydney rivalry coming through). Growing up on Origin, I've seen some of the greatest players in the game come through and become household names – names like Darren Lockyer, Billy Slater and Cameron Smith (or Allan Langer, Wally Lewis and Andrew Johns for the NSW supporters). But one player who draws more respect than most is Mal Meninga. Named as one of the 100 Greatest Players in the game, Meninga was an iconic player in Australian football and remains one of the top point scorers in State of Origin history, among many other accolades.

What I love about Mal's story is that after he retired from the field he went on to coach the Queensland State of Origin team to a record-breaking nine title wins from ten series, in the most successful Origin coaching stint in NRL history. He shifted seamlessly from star player to 'raising stars'. Investing in others didn't reduce his credibility; if anything it made it stronger.

If you want to build your credibility as a leader, you need to take time to intentionally build the community of people who follow you; coach, mentor and develop the community of followers you have built.

Consistency

Get better at helping others.

Consistency is one of the most underrated values of great leaders. I think we should shine a light on it a lot more often than we do. Cassandra currently works for one of Australia's leading not-for-profit organisations here in Victoria. She often tells me stories of the volunteers who are recognised for their long service in the organisation. These volunteers may have been serving the organisation for anywhere from 15 to 50 years. That type of consistency is rare, and extraordinarily valuable.

The word 'consistency' has its origins in the Latin word *consistere*, which means to stand firm or stand still and endure, and ultimately that's how credibility is built, through endurance and unwavering commitment. I have a lot of respect for leaders who have determined what it is they want to be known for and who have stood firm and committed themselves to that.

Leaders with strong credibility have consistently invested in the development of those they lead. They have determined who they are and what they know or do, and they have not wavered from that. That isn't to say that consistency is at war with change. It is possible to be consistent in your positioning while at the same time growing, adapting and evolving. If you are a healthy leader you are always growing, and if you are growing you are changing.

Consistency is about determining who you want to be and standing firm on that while adapting what you do. Take a look at one of the world's most trusted brands, Coca-Cola. We are talking about an organisation that has grown and evolved since the late 1800s to become what it is today, with all kinds of products in different categories. Yet in their growth and evolution the brand has stayed true to its message of fun, friends and good times. Their communication is more than just their product; it is a consistent message of *happiness*.

Credibility

Be known for what you have done and how you help others.

The most credible leaders I know have a legacy of credibility. They have spent years, even decades, becoming known for what they have built and how they have helped others to do the same. They aren't just great leaders in their own right, but great leaders *of* leaders. They haven't just built empires for themselves, but have helped others build their own empires. They haven't pursued credibility as much as they have remained consistent over time and in turn have been recognised for it.

There is no shortage of talented and capable leaders, but leaders who have stood the test of time without compromise, who have built credibility through their consistent investment in others are rare. That is the reason their words carry weight and why people will lean forward in their seats to listen to them. It's the reason people will come from across the world to hear them speak, or part with large sums of money to sit with them and learn for just a few hours.

It bears repeating: talent may be what gets you a platform, but credibility will give you a voice that people will listen to.

You might be starting to freak out just little here, thinking to yourself, *I haven't built that kind of credibility, so nobody will want to listen to me*. Not true. People who have worked on building credibility will have an advantage over new communicators and leaders. It takes time and consistency to communicate with that kind of weight, but if you do the work, that can become your reality too.

I have a close friend named Jose who is a branding genius, and I don't use that word lightly. Every time I speak with him, his thinking in this space elevates my perspective. He was sharing a journey he had taken a client of his on, and I couldn't help but think of it passing through the five credibility levels.

His client was an incredible artist and designer. He had spent years investing in his craft, improving and showcasing his work, developing a respectable online following through his social media account. As their numbers started to grow he engaged Jose and his agency to help him find a way to turn this into a business.

He was in the contribution stage. He had developed and improved his craft and was investing his talent and making a valuable contribution to the artistic community. He would regularly upload videos speaking at events and showcasing his talent at creative conferences. He partnered with large brands and began to amass a large following, and he was often recognised for his contribution in the space.

When Jose began to work with the artist he had built a strong following of admirers. But Jose knew that if he was going to build credibility in this space he needed to do more than just be good. He needed to help others be good. Jose began to help him shift from being *an artist* to being *a mentor to artists*. He started sharing tutorial videos and selling the brushes he used. He began to re-post emerging artists' posts and showcase their work alongside his own. He started to build an online community of people he helped become better. Today he continues to invest in the community he has built and to find new and innovative ways to do so. No longer just a great artist, he now has a new level of credibility among artists and that is adding weight to the way he communicates.

Don't just commit to developing your talent. Build your credibility.

CHAPTER 4
MANAGE YOUR REPUTATION

Reputation speaks before you do. Whether you realise it or not, you are already speaking long before you stand up at the front of the room.

At the beginning of 2018, when I was hosting a Q&A on one of my social media channels, I was asked, 'When you start speaking to a new crowd that don't know you, how do you build connection and rapport?'

Without much thought I prepared a response that ran through a few techniques you could adopt to help build rapport and connection with your audience. These included the usual things, like telling a relevant personal story or finding someone who is well known by the crowd to introduce you. Then I stopped myself and thought a bit deeper about the question and my experience. I've found that just because someone doesn't know me doesn't mean they haven't heard of me. And it sure doesn't mean they can't learn about me in just a few moments or clicks.

We live in a globally connected society with easier access to more information than ever before. When I tell people that the GFC was a game changer, I don't mean the Global Financial

Crisis. I'm talking about the Google Fact Check. Do you remember the good old days when you used to *trust* people. They would tell you something and you would just *believe* them. Now you can't say something without people immediately grabbing their phones to verify.

What makes you think people aren't doing the same to 'verify' you? There is a wealth of information that people can learn about you before you even walk through the door, let alone stand on a platform. If you have had the opportunity to stand in front of a room full of strangers, there's a good chance they know more about you than you think.

A valuable element of positioning is understanding what people are already saying about you. It's knowing what kind of reputation you have in the minds of your audience. There are certain moments I have found valuable to leverage. These are the kinds of moments that will help you manage your reputation and ensure the picture people have of you in their mind reflects the positioning you want to create.

SIX KEY MOMENTS

Figure 5 shows the six key moments that every leader can leverage to help manage their reputation before they stand up to speak.

Figure 5: Key moments in reputation management

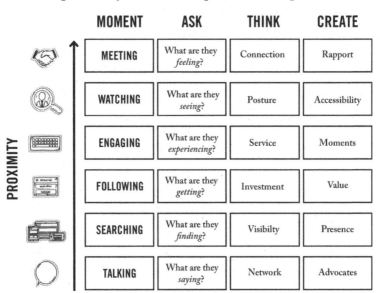

PROXIMITY	MOMENT	ASK	THINK	CREATE
	MEETING	What are they *feeling?*	Connection	Rapport
	WATCHING	What are they *seeing?*	Posture	Accessibility
	ENGAGING	What are they *experiencing?*	Service	Moments
	FOLLOWING	What are they *getting?*	Investment	Value
	SEARCHING	What are they *finding?*	Visibilty	Presence
	TALKING	What are they *saying?*	Network	Advocates

Talking

People are talking about you.

In boardrooms and at barbecues, in your staff meetings and around the water cooler, people are talking about you. People who don't know you personally will likely know someone who does. The question you need to ask is, what are they saying? What does the conversation sound like when your name comes up? Is it positive or negative? Are people telling good stories or bad?

As a leader you need to think about your *network*, because your network is how you influence a conversation you're not part of. You leverage this moment when you tap into the power of your network and create *advocates*. Advocates are those people who will speak well of you when you aren't present. I like to think of them as guardians of your reputation.

Searching

People are searching for you online.

They are using what they find to build a picture of who you are and what you are about. We've all been guilty from time to time of a little light social media stalking. Don't deny it, we've seen you on the 'who's viewed your profile' list. The question you need to ask is, *what are they finding?*

If I read your LinkedIn bio, what would I learn about who you are and what you value? When I check out your staff profile on the intranet or read your website bio, who is the person I find? When I take a look at your social media feed on Twitter or Facebook, will this tell the story you want me to read?

At a conference I recently facilitated one of the guest speakers was to talk about how to create 'healthy' leadership, a topic I was obviously very interested in hearing about. Not many of us had heard him speak before, so naturally people started looking him up. Not long before he was due to speak one of the group chats I was in pinged with a notification. I looked down and saw that someone had posted a link to a news article about the speaker. The article didn't paint the speaker in a great light with respect to his treatment of his employees. Here was someone about to speak on *healthy* leadership, and this is the reputation that preceded him?

I should pause for a moment and say that I'm not one to take at face value every online news article, and I think our world is for the most part savvy enough to know when the media is just being, well, the media. What struck me, though, was that before he had said a word, his reputation had set him up to be viewed in a particular way. So he was already starting on the back foot and had to work more intentionally to have his voice heard.

As a leader you need to think about your *visibility*. How are you showing up in the places people are looking for you? How can you be more intentional about creating a *presence* online? Are you actively engaging in the places where people are looking? Could you write regularly on topics you want to be known for and align your social media pages with your message? If you're speaking externally, think about how you might show up in the conference hashtag, write guest articles for the event and put yourself in front of the delegates any way you can.

Following

People are following you online.

People are reading your online content and seeing your status updates. When you send an angry tweet because your flight is delayed, your team and your audience see that too. So what does this all say about you?

The question I often ask myself is, *What are they getting by following me?* Have I given them a reason to follow? Why would someone want to read your staff newsletter or online articles or follow your tweets?

As a leader you need to think *investment*. How can you use what you have to invest in those you lead? Find opportunities to create *value* for the people who follow you before they even meet you. Give them a good reason to keep following you. Be generous with ideas and resources and continue to help them solve real problems, and you'll build a great reputation long before you have the opportunity to communicate directly.

Engaging

People are engaging with you.

Whether it's through an online comment or email or over the phone, the question to ask is, *what are they experiencing when they do?* When they ask a question, send you an email or share one of your articles, what is your response? Are you often late responding to emails? Are you short and abrupt when sending messages? Do you sometimes not return phone calls? These actions are shaping your reputation.

As a leader think with a *service* mindset, just as you would want every one of your employees to do with your customers. How can you create *moments* that are memorable for people who engage with you? How can you surprise and delight your team or audience? How can you do something they won't quickly forget when they finally see you in person.

Watching

When you show up to speak, know that people are watching you from across the room, they are standing beside you in the elevator, they are in front of you in the coffee line. You might not know them or even see them, but they see you (insert eerie horror music). That person you just glared at or flipped the bird to may just be the new employee starting in your organisation today, who will build a picture of the type of person you are from such interactions. When you walk down the hall on your lunch break and ignore your team, you need to know that people notice.

What are they seeing? What is your *posture* when you enter a room? Do you come across as arrogant, disconnected and closed off, or approachable, friendly and humble? Does your expression suggest you want to be there or does it say *stand clear*? Do all you can to create *accessibility* for people to connect with you. Utilise your preparation time privately, so you can maximise your connection time publicly. Rather than just going through your notes, make the most of those valuable moments you have before you speak. When you're *in* the room, you're *on*.

Meeting

People are meeting you before you speak.

People are looking for opportunities to connect with you. The question to ask is, *what are they feeling when they do eventually meet you?*

Do they feel valued and important or do they walk away feeling like they were an inconvenience to you? Keep in mind that 'people don't care how much you know until they know how much you care'. How are you showing people through your interactions that you care? Maybe you've met them in the hallway between meetings, in the lobby before a town hall or in the car park on your way home.

Think about *connection* and look for opportunities to create *rapport* with your audience before you stand up to speak. I have learned that every one of these moments is a valuable opportunity to position yourself in the way that you want to be known. Take a minute to reflect on these moments that help you to speak before you speak and ask yourself, are you saying something valuable?

SPEAK BEYOND THE ROOM

When you do speak, you are never just speaking to the people in the room.

In recently released figures on device use in Australia, the NBN Co reported:

> *'The average Australian home has 13.7 connected devices within its walls, ranging from obvious candidates like mobile phones, tablets, video game consoles and eBook readers, to increasingly more bespoke technology. Telsyte's research predicts that the average Australian home will have 30.7 connected*

devices by the year 2021, which would be an overall growth of 124% in just four years.'

If you say something in the room, you will need to be prepared for how it could be shared beyond the room and in turn how that might impact your reputation.

In 2006 the American actor Michael Richards, 'Kramer' in the hit television sitcom *Seinfeld*, came under heavy scrutiny for an incident that took place at The Laugh Factory in Hollywood. In a video Richards was seen hurling angry racial insults at a group of African-American patrons after a heckling incident. He later apologised publicly for the outburst. Unfortunately, much of the damage to his reputation was done after the video went viral.

As a leader, when you stand in front of a room it's easy to imagine that anything you say inside those four walls will remain there, but that's a dangerous presumption. *Everything* you say has the potential to make or break your reputation.

At the end of 2018 I was invited to speak at a team gathering for a local council here in Victoria. When I arrived, I was seated at a table at the front of the room next to a man I had never met. I took a moment to introduce myself and he spoke to me in a very familiar way, as though he had met me before. This was more than possible, given that I had spent the past year speaking at all kinds of conferences and events, but of course I started to feel bad that I didn't recognise him. A short while into our conversation I asked him if he had ever heard me speak before. He smiled and said, 'I sure have. I heard you speak earlier this year at an event for finance professionals'. I remembered the event and felt relieved we hadn't actually met personally. Then I asked him whether he enjoyed my presentation. 'I did,' he replied, as he took out his phone and opened a recording app. 'I recorded it and gave it to my manager.'

For a moment my heart sank as I thought back to that presentation and what I had said. I had become a little relaxed about what I shared with the room, but this was an important reminder. You never know who is listening to what you say, or even recording it to share with others.

THE DANGER OF DISTANCE

The danger of distance is that the further we get from the source the more distorted our interpretation can become.

When my wife and I travelled to Italy in 2018 we visited Florence and decided to take a guided tour through the Galleria dell'Accademia to see the Statue of David. To be honest we only took the tour because we didn't want to wait in the queues, but one of the great benefits of guided tours is that you often learn stories and facts you likely wouldn't hear of if you went independently. One of the stories that stood out for me related to the proportions of David's hands and head. If you have ever seen the statue, you may not have noticed this, but they are unusually large in comparison to the rest of the body. The proportions seem to be distorted. Was Michelangelo, the great sculptor, drunk when he carved this? Was it a mistake? Actually, the guide explained to us, the statue was intended to be placed high up on the cathedral roof. Given this elevated position, these features were deliberately exaggerated to allow for the viewers' perspective.

Whenever you communicate as a leader you need to think about how your message will be perceived by people outside the room. How should you frame your message to reduce the risk of it being distorted? How can you be more intentional with language to avoid misinterpretation? How will this message translate across different contexts and cultures? KFC may have thought their slogan 'finger lickin' good' would work just fine at the launch into the Chinese market, but when it was translated as 'eat your fingers off' they fell prey to the danger of distance.

I like to think of it as like radio waves radiating out from the source (see Figure 6). Consider how quickly distance can distort your message and impact your reputation, and what you can do to reduce that risk.

Figure 6: Amplifying Your Message

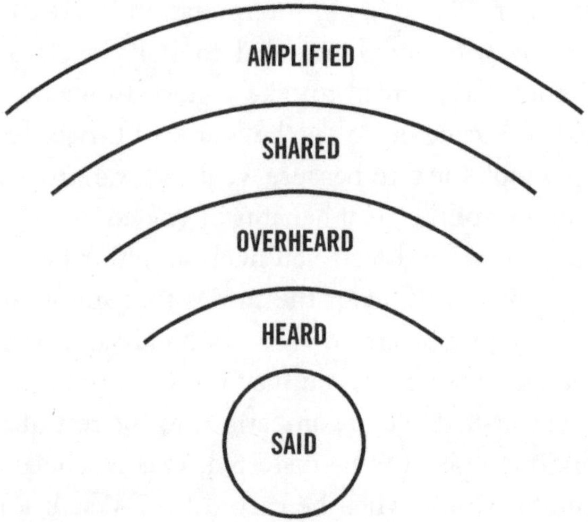

A message is *said* with an original intent.

That same message is *heard* with an interpretation.

Then it's shared by one person to another and in the process *overheard*, and reinterpreted or misinterpreted, without the context.

That message is then *shared* with a group.

Those who receive the message then share it widely, so the message is *amplified* to a larger audience.

In 2013 a PR executive from New York City learned a harsh lesson when a tweet sent to her 170 followers before boarding a flight to Africa went viral. It read: 'Going to Africa. Hope I don't get AIDS. Just kidding. I'm white.'

A tweet that was made in jest was sent with a desired intent within the context of her small social circle. In an interview with *The New York Times Magazine* she wrote:

> *'Living in America puts us in a bit of a bubble when it comes to what is going on in the third world. I was making fun of that bubble. To me it was so insane of a comment for anyone to make, I thought there was no way that anyone could possibly think it was literal.'*

Unfortunately, sharing those few ill-chosen words would have significant consequences for her life and reputation, all within the timeframe of an 11-hour flight.

You can learn from a story like this how quickly a message we communicate can escalate and damage a reputation. In this case:

A message is conveyed to a small group of people.

The message is interpreted differently by the audience.

That message is shared with a journalist, who in turn shares it with a larger following.

That larger following shares a misinterpretation, which is amplified though social media.

That message, with its own hashtag, is now trending across Twitter.

The original tweeter's reputation is damaged.

I do feel the need to qualify this story with a couple of comments. Firstly, that tweet was ridiculous, and I have no doubt the person who shared it knows that and with hindsight would not have sent it. Undoubtedly if you share something like that it is likely to be misinterpreted. I feel deeply saddened for this person who had to suffer under the weight of that bad choice. It is an unfortunate example of the danger of distance. Reputation is easily damaged and hard, though not impossible, to restore. But it is worth repeating Stephen Covey's observation, 'You can't talk your way out of a problem you behaved your way into'. If you damage your reputation through what you have said, you can't just talk your way out of it; you'll need to *walk* your way out of it, and that takes a lot of hard work. Better to guard your reputation than to find yourself having to rebuild it.

The moment you say something publicly, or sometimes even under the cloak of privacy, that information is out in the world and has the potential to be distorted and amplified. The principle here is quite simple:

If you aren't prepared for something you say to be potentially distorted and amplified, consider whether you should actually say it.

You won't always be able to control whether or not people misinterpret what you say, but there is a lot of work you can do to reduce the likelihood of your being misread. That starts with getting clarity in your key message and delivering it in a way that is easy to understand, which is what we will explore in the next part of this book.

PART 2
MESSAGING

Great communicators obsess about *messaging*, because great communication is more than just saying something; it's having something *valuable* to say.

Have you ever sat in the audience during a presentation, thinking to yourself, *I have no idea what he/she is trying to say?* Or maybe you've walked away from a team meeting or town hall and wished you could reclaim the time you've just wasted. Or perhaps, at the other end of the spectrum, the speaker is dumping so many thoughts and ideas on you that you feel overwhelmed and walk away struggling to recall even one of them.

In the mid 2000s there was a television series called *Thank God You're Here*. It was one of my favourite shows, which was surprising given that I feel sick in my stomach watching someone else feel publicly embarrassed or uncomfortable. For those who missed it, the premise of the show was that celebrities or comedians were dropped into a fictitious scene for which they had no context or preparation. As they entered the room, one of the improvisation actors would deliver the opening line, 'Thank God you're here', which was their cue to start the scene. It was hilarious to watch the victim try to make sense of their surroundings and improvise their way through. The thing you could always be sure of with this show was that you had no idea where it would go.

I've incorporated a version of this activity in some of my training workshops and I love using one scenario in particular. I start by asking one person to leave the room, and after they have left I tell the others they have now miraculously become journalists and reporters. I let them know they are about to interview the team captain and winner of the Sydney to Hobart yacht race fresh off their latest victory. The only catch is they aren't allowed to ask questions that give away what the press conference is about. They can ask only vague, generic questions like 'How does it feel to win?' or 'What was the key to your success?'

Over time I have had some interesting questions and some hilarious answers. One of my favourites was the question 'Can you talk us through your weekly training regime?', which prompted the response 'It usually starts with practising in my pool in the backyard'. The direction and answers differ every time I run this activity, but it's always a lot of fun. I should note that it has worked 99.9 per cent of the time. The exception was a guy named Steve, who actually had the Sydney to Hobart in his mind and guessed the scenario immediately. Among the program participants he became known as *Psychic Steve*.

While it just seems like fun for the participants, there is actually a deeper purpose behind the exercise. When I ask participants afterwards to describe how it felt to stand in front of the room and navigate the scenario, I usually get quite similar responses:

- 'I had no idea what I was supposed to say.'

- 'I thought I was answering questions about one thing, then everything changed when I was asked a different question.'

- 'I felt like I couldn't go deep on anything because I didn't know if what I was saying was relevant.'

- 'It felt like I was going all over the place.'

- When I asked them what would have made the activity easier, again I found people responding in similar ways:

- 'Knowing what I was supposed to be talking about, of course!'

- 'Having some time to prepare what I was going to say.'

- 'Knowing who I was speaking to and what they wanted from me.'

These are all perfectly normal responses. Of course it is going to be easier to speak when you have taken time to understand why you are speaking, what you have to say and how you will say it in an impactful way.

I remind the people I work with regularly that there is a big difference between saying something and having something valuable to say. Everyone can speak, but not everything is worth listening to. Speaking without taking the time to understand and develop your *message* is like trying to drive a bus without a steering wheel: you'll just find yourself moving in the direction of the bus's momentum.

Messaging is the obsession that sits at the intersection of knowing *what* you want to say and knowing *how* to deliver it with the greatest impact. In Part 2 we will explore three messaging activities that every leader should actively engage in:

1. **Determine the value** – What are you speaking for?

2. **Define your message** – What do you want to say?

3. **Deliver with impact** – How will you say it?

In these chapters I will take you through the process I use every time I prepare to present. I have used this tool to help many capture and communicate their thoughts in an impactful way. Occasionally I am asked the question 'If you say we should be authentic and do what is natural to us, then how will following someone else's process enable us to do that?' It's a valid question. My response takes the form of a different question: 'How did you learn to ride a bike?' Most likely while you were learning you started with training wheels. Then you began to pedal along with someone walking beside you to help you course-correct when in danger of hitting a tree. Eventually you found what worked for you and you decided the direction you would go in the most natural way. What I'm about to share is simply a process to support you as you build your confidence. Over time, through practice, you will find what is natural to you and learn what does and doesn't work for you. First, though, I suggest you commit to trusting the process and taking the time to get out and give it a go.

CHAPTER 5
DETERMINE THE VALUE

People don't just listen *because* you speak. They listen when you give them a *reason* to.

Whether you are implementing change, navigating your way through a crisis or trying to build and shape your culture, you need to give people a reason to listen to what you have to say. You do so by showing them you have something of *value* to them.

We live in a world of work in which time is a scarce commodity. Ask someone how their week has been, and the most likely response you'll get is 'Busy'. When people choose to give up a slice of their time, there is an unspoken expectation that they will receive some kind of value in exchange. If you've ever been in a meeting that could have been covered in an email or sat in a town hall to receive updates that could have been conveyed in a short conversation, then you would have experienced the frustration that results when your time isn't valued.

As you start your preparation journey you'll need to consider your reason for speaking. Is your message better suited to an email or to face-to face delivery? If face to face, how can you best deliver value to the people you are speaking to.

Let's look at three ways you can add value every time you step up on your platform to speak.

SOLVE PROBLEMS

Regina Brett once wrote, 'If we all threw our problems in a pile and saw everyone else's, we'd probably grab ours back'. Or, in the words of songwriter Julia Michaels, 'I got issues, but you got 'em too'. While we may all be different in many ways, one thing is for sure: we've all got problems, big or small, that we'd like to solve. If you can do that for me, you have delivered value.

When I was studying for my postgraduate degree in Counselling, I learned to distinguish between different types of problems. In psychology they are described as the *presenting problem* and the *real problem*. This isn't to suggest that a presenting problem isn't a real problem, but rather that a presenting problem tends to be the fruit of an issue rather than the root of an issue. Some are surface-level problems; others resonate at a deeper level.

I am now part of an incredible tribe of leaders orbiting round the Thought Leaders Business School. In this program I have heard founders Matt Church and Peter Cook describe these problems as the 'known spoken' and the 'known unspoken'. Known spoken problems are those that people talk openly about with one another. I like to think of it as like the game show *Family Feud* where the host declares 'We surveyed 100 people about _____, and the top 10 answers were...' The known unspoken is more likely to be the one-to-one conversation you would have when you open up and reveal what's really going on inside your head, probably over a nice glass of Pinot.

When I work with leaders to help them determine the value they have when they speak, I describe these concepts in the form of a metaphor. I ask them to think about:

- the boardroom
- the bedroom.

The boardroom problems I ask them to describe are the known spoken or the presenting problems. What are the problems that your employees would talk about openly around the boardroom table in a meeting if you asked them to? If, as on *Family Feud*, you surveyed 100 of your employees, what would the top 10 answers be?

Now take a moment to think about the bedroom problems (yes, I'm aware how that sounds and yes, I'm okay with that). What are the problems that keep them up at night, the problems they think about a lot but are scared to share? These are the known unspoken and the 'real problems'.

Let's take a look at an example. Imagine you need to lead your team through an organisational restructure. What are some of the boardroom and bedroom problems that your team might be thinking about (see table below)?

BOARDROOM	BEDROOM
• What does this mean for my job now? • I don't like change. • Will I get along with my new team leader?	• What if I can't provide for my family? • Is there a future for me here? • Why do I bother showing up?

If you want to deliver a message that counts, it all starts with an awareness and understanding of these problems and knowing how to address them when you speak.

ANSWER QUESTIONS

One of the mantras I share with leaders who have to speak is simply this: *Don't answer a question that nobody in the room is asking.* There's very little that is engaging about giving people an answer to a question they didn't ask and don't care about. If you believe the question is important, then you need to start by taking your audience on a journey that evokes that question, causing them to ask it in their own mind. Alternatively you could take a moment to consider the key questions your audience is already asking.

For example, if your staff have never heard you talk about the vision for your company, chances are they are asking questions like 'Where are we going?', 'What are we working towards?' and 'What's important to our leaders?' And going deeper you will probably find bigger questions like 'Do I want to be here?' and 'Why do I bother to show up?'

One of my favourite quotes is from Madeleine L'Engle:

> *'The minute we begin to think we have all the answers,*
> *we forget the questions.'*

You add value when you help your audience answer the questions they are asking in their mind.

RELIEVE TENSIONS

We will explore the principle of tension further in chapter 7, but being able to create and relieve tension is an art every leader and speaker should master. Hollywood is in the business of creating and relieving tension in the minds of the audience to keep them actively engaged in the narrative. Will that perfect couple get together? Will the hero defeat the enemy and save the day? Who was the killer?

I have found myself dragged into the abyss of binge viewing a whole Netflix series purely because of this principle. Every time I watch an episode, I tell myself it will be the last one, but then it ends on *such* a cliffhanger... Of course I can't stop there without knowing what happens next, and so the cycle continues. Tension is ultimately about creating forces that act in opposition to each other. A desired end state seems eternally out of reach because of the insuperable obstacles to achieving it, yet we have a deep need for resolution and release.

Great songwriting builds on a foundation of musical tension and release. There are moments in great songs that elicit a kind of euphoria when the tension built is finally released. It's the moment everyone waits for, when the drums hit in 'In the Air Tonight' by Phil Collins, when the bass finally drops in an Avicii remix, or when every person in the room screams, in a different key, 'You're the voice try and understand it'! A few years ago a video that went viral featured a song that continued to build up tension but offered no resolution. Many expressed indignant frustration because the tension wasn't resolved or relieved. Parody artists The Lonely Island released a song titled 'When Will the Bass Drop?' that illustrates the same point. Great music balances tension and release to create engagement and satisfaction.

George Loewenstein, a behavioural economist at Carnegie Mellon University, describes curiosity as what happens when we feel a gap in our knowledge. That knowledge gap ultimately creates and causes us pain, and we must fill the gap to relieve the pain. It's why many of us try so hard to figure out the ending of the movie before it happens. The tension created by our inability to close that gap in knowledge is what keeps us engaged through the movie until the end (or takes us straight to the spoiler page).

If you want people to listen. Give them a reason to by adding value:

- When implementing change, add value by helping people understand how this change will solve their or the company's problems.

- When creating clarity out of uncertainty, add value by resolving the internal tension people feel about the uncertainty.

- When shaping culture, add value by answering the question people are always asking: 'How do we do things here?'

When you lead with a desire to add value for the people you are speaking to, you demonstrate that you value *them*. You tell them you care about their time, you appreciate that they showed up and you want to leave them in a better place than where you found them.

CHAPTER 6
DEFINE YOUR MESSAGE

Never underestimate the *big* impact of a few *small* words.

I recently spoke at a conference for corporate communications professionals in Sydney. I was fortunate to be able to sit in on one of the sessions with a member of the team from Microsoft in Asia when he shared some of the Microsoft story. He was of course a proud ambassador of the company and was speaking at a great time for them, having just learned that Microsoft had overtaken Apple as the world's most valuable company. (Since the two rivals have continued to trade back and forth.) While I knew a small part of the story, I realised during his presentation that there was so much more to it that I was unaware of. One powerful moment that stood out for me was the journey of Microsoft's current CEO, Satya Nadella, since he stepped into the role in 2014.

While Microsoft was and is known predominantly for its Windows operating system (and had it to thank for much of the company's growth under former CEOs Bill Gates and Steve Ballmer), in his first public appearance Nadella focused instead on a different key idea – *the cloud*. It was a bold break with the priorities of his predecessors, but he wanted the world and his employees to know that under his leadership Microsoft was going to embrace the cloud and have their technology running across all platforms.

He reimagined the company's mission statement, which eventually became 'to empower every person and organisation on the planet to achieve more'. Simple and yet profound. This message was communicated widely and reinforced across every level of the organisation. It's hard to imagine there is an employee anywhere in Microsoft who couldn't tell you what their company's mission statement is today.

Under Steve Ballmer's 14 years of leadership Microsoft's stock prices had mostly shifted sideways, yet in the five years since Nadella took the reins Microsoft's share price almost tripled, a comeback story that has made headlines globally.

One small word, *cloud*, and a new, concise mission statement. One huge impact.

I'm not suggesting that Microsoft's success was the direct result of clearly defining their message. Obviously you need to be able to deliver on your promise and have powerful strategy and execution to see this type of turnaround. But when it comes to mobilising a workforce, these were the words that set a course and framed the future direction of the company under Nadella, and it was that change of direction that resulted in the company's great success.

Working with leaders to define their message I have a simple mantra: *Start with clarity and end with simplicity.* Get clear on what it is you want to say, then do the hard work to find the simplest way to say it.

START WITH CLARITY

Ambiguity is a breeding ground for complexity. When we don't know the one thing we *must* say, we end up focusing on all the things we *could* say and making it difficult for people to take anything away.

While reading Chip and Dan Heath's book *Made to Stick*, one concept was a standout to me. It's called *Commanders Intent* (CI), which they describe as 'a crisp, plain talk statement that appears at the top of every order, specifying the plan's goal, the desired end-state of an operation'.

In essence, CI is a simple and clear statement of what success looks like. As it gets passed down the chain of command, layers of strategy and tactics are added, but the intent is always clear. This perfectly illustrates the priority of getting clear on what is most important before speaking. Here in Australia, though, I have learned that American concepts don't always translate well, so I sent a message to a friend of mine who lectures in Leadership and Ethics at the Royal Military College in Canberra. I wanted to ask him about this concept and how it looks here in Australia. His response:

> *'We do actually use, and love, Commander's Intent in the Australian Army too. We use it in a broad number of ways, usually for orders or back briefs. The way we do it is by stating our Purpose, Method and End State. This can be holistic or just for a phase or component of a task or project. Method provides the most details, though the whole thing rarely takes more than a minute to provide. The idea is that you don't have to go crazy with the detail if your team knows what you're trying to achieve.'*

I love that last thought. Most people I work with who have issues with over-speaking or finding themselves talking in circles do so because they haven't taken the time to get clear on their intent. I have learned that when you can get clear on your intent, you'll have much more impact with your content.

When a leader is preparing to speak I will often ask them to tell me what they need to communicate in less than 60 seconds. If they can't succinctly articulate one clear message they need to get across, then I know there is work to be done. It's easy to get a message across in 60 minutes; the challenge is getting it across in one.

To start with clarity, decide on your goal:

- What I want people to know or do is _____.

- If nothing else, I want people to remember _____.

- What matters most is that people _____.

You need to get your big idea down on paper. Like a north bearing on a compass, it's going to help you chart a course for the rest of your content. And by getting clarity around your message you will have a better understanding of what to keep and what to cut. I have found that one of the biggest challenges for leaders is not about what they should *add* to their presentation, but what they should *remove* from it.

Michelangelo is one of history's greatest artists, yet to this day his creative process remains mysterious. Admiring his Statue of David in Florence, I couldn't imagine how he could have approached such a creative challenge. Our guide shared with us that Michelangelo would often create in isolation, so we have very limited information on his method. But from the little that is known, she explained, his process has come to be described as the 'art of subtraction'. The artist believed that 'the sculpture already existed within the marble block and that it was his job to chisel away everything that was not necessary in order to reveal it'.

Taking the time to gain clarity with your message makes the art of subtraction so much easier. It means removing everything unnecessary or unhelpful to reveal a clear idea or message that is valuable to your audience.

I have found the hardest part of the process isn't finding the content or information to share but knowing what brings it all together, finding the common thread that connects each piece you share. There's nothing wrong with communicating a number of big points, as long as each of those points helps to build and reinforce the one central idea you want people to remember. Your points may be great, but they won't be what people remember.

It's easy to fall into the habit of *addition*. You start with a great idea or topic but find that as you gather all your thoughts and source all the information, you lose clarity and end up staring at a giant mass of content. We've all been there.

You can find yourself caught up in the addition trap if:

- you can't succinctly articulate one clear message or tie content together

- you find yourself obsessing about how you might fill the timeslot

- you have too much content for your allocated time

- you have multiple different directions you could go in.

The big question to keep asking yourself throughout the preparation process is simple: 'Does this *reveal* or does it *conceal* my key message or idea?' If it helps people understand your message or it clarifies the big idea, then keep it. If it distracts, conceals or diverts people from your key message, cut it out.

Don't be afraid of speaking less or coming in under your allocated time. People rarely complain about finishing early. Be more concerned about sharing one clear message and conveying it to your audience in such a way that they will never forget it.

END WITH SIMPLICITY

Tricia Brouk, an award-winning director, writer and TEDx producer, argues the case for brevity and simplicity in an *HBR* article titled 'To Give a Great Presentation, Distill Your Message to Just 15 Words'. I often ask the people I work with to tell me in 15 words or fewer what the key message of their presentation is? If they can't I leave them to continue the work and come back to me when they've got there, or we workshop it together.

Haddon Robinson, a Dallas Theological Seminary professor, once told a room full of emerging church ministers, 'If it's a mist in the pulpit, it's a fog in the pews'. If, as a leader, you cannot articulate the message you want to share simply and succinctly, it's extremely unlikely to be clear to the people listening. Remember that *simple* does not mean *simplistic*, but it does mean memorable.

Why does this matter? It matters because people will struggle to *practise* what they cannot *remember*, and the goal of every leader is not just to speak so that people listen, it's to lead so that people change.

When I first started getting opportunities to speak and lead people from a platform, I would sometimes be stopped by people in the street who recognised me. It was a strange feeling that someone knew about me, yet we had never met. I remember one time being stopped by a young woman while walking through Melbourne's CBD. She struck up a conversation before introducing me to her boss. All I could find myself thinking was *who is this person?* You do everything in those moments not to embarrass the other person, all the while racking your brain to connect the dots. A few weeks later I ran into her again, this time alone, and she said, 'I'm sorry, I realised you don't actually know me, but I'm one of the volunteers. I see you speak regularly and just wanted to say hi'.

One of my favourite experiences is when someone stops me in the street and shares a story about something I said that in some way influenced their life. When it first happened I was surprised and humbled. Now when people stop me and share stories of things I said three or four years ago, I feel the full extent and impact of memorable messaging.

Take a moment to think about some of the most inspirational presentations you have heard. Without going to your notes, what were they about? They usually happen in moments that matter for you, and there was likely one big idea that stood out and resonated with you and that you still remember. Such inspiration is not limited to presentations, of course. Almost everyone I speak to can recall a moment when someone they respected said something to them that influenced their life, most often (but not always) in a positive way. Or perhaps it was a book that communicated one clear message that resonated and stuck with you. One thing is certain: if you want to influence people, you need to convey a message that is clear and easy to remember.

We'll explore what you can do to make your message memorable in later chapters, but the key message here is to *start with clarity and end with simplicity*. Find what you want to say then determine how you can say it in the most impactful and memorable way.

CHAPTER 7
DELIVER WITH IMPACT

So you have something valuable to say. How do you say it?

I know, you're thinking, *Finally we're getting to the heart of it. At last we're going to talk about how to actually stand up and deliver.* But I hope by now you are starting to understand that there is much more to communicating a *message that counts* than just how it's delivered.

I've had the privilege of presenting from platforms in a variety of different formats and contexts. I've spoken in lounge rooms to five people, boardrooms to 15 and on stages to 1,500, yet my process remains mostly unchanged. What I'm about to share is my process for capturing and communicating my thoughts with impact.

I'm not for a moment going to suggest that this is the only way to deliver with impact, nor that I have discovered the Holy Grail of effective communication. What I do have is a process that works for me and has helped many of the people I work with achieve a lot more impact with a lot less effort. Processes are designed to release you, not restrict you. They should make your planning process simpler and more streamlined. They are not about blocking your creative expression or pre-empting your original thinking.

I have a friend, Leonie, who is *a really great human being*. She works in community aid and development and has spent years in the not-for-profit sector helping disadvantaged people from all walks of life. There are a few people in my life who regularly challenge and enlarge my thinking in different ways, and Leonie definitely does this for me in the space of social justice. One of my favourite stories, though, is actually about an experience she had at a café.

Leonie, being who she is, brings her 'keep cup' with her whenever she goes out for a coffee. Being more environmentally responsible than most of us, she consciously avoids single-use cups. One time she went to a café to order coffee and handed over her keep cup to the person behind the counter and gave her order, whereupon the staff member reached over and grabbed a paper cup from the pile and proceeded to write Leonie's name and order on the cup before placing it inside the glass keep cup and handing it to the barista. As you can imagine, Leonie questioned this behaviour, only to be told that this is how they keep track of the orders. Of course the cup is then thrown out, essentially rendering the keep cup completely redundant. This story always makes me laugh because it perfectly illustrates the danger of blindly following a process without thought.

My goal here isn't to give you a process to follow blindly, but to provide a framework for you to adapt to your own context. It's the scaffolding around the building. What you build within that is up to you. Nobody knows your people as you do, so as you navigate this process, do so with intentional thinking, applying it to your own particular context.

THE FLIGHT PATH STRUCTURE

As my practice has grown it has inevitably meant more travel. I've mentioned that I have always struggled with flying, but

I have learned to appreciate its advantages – all that it enables me to do and all the places it helps me get to. Over time the experience has become less daunting because for the most part I know just what to expect.

An announcement over the public address system invites you to board the plane, after which you stow your carry-on bag and settle into your seat. Once all the pre-flight checks and safety demonstrations are completed the plane pushes back and begins to taxi down the runway. Finally the aircraft takes off and ascends to cruising altitude. You sit back and enjoy the view (if you have one) and while away the hours to your destination. Eventually the seatbelt sign comes back on as you descend and make a smooth landing (usually) before disembarking at the end of your journey. The standard process, in a nutshell, is:

- boarding
- departing
- flying
- landing
- disembarking.

Repeat this process enough times and even anxious travellers find that it becomes easier to get their head in the right place. It isn't too long before you actually learn to enjoy it. You think less about the process, and the journey becomes a lot more natural and comfortable. I have mentioned a few times in the course of this book that communication is an incredibly powerful vehicle to help move and mobilise people from where they are to where we need them to be. I find it helpful to think about this process as much like air travel. We take people on a journey from one point to another. While we might be nervous the first few times, with much repetition the journey becomes a lot less stressful. Do it enough times and it even becomes enjoyable.

On a recent flight, during our ascent the plane hit unexpected turbulence, my least favourite part of the experience. I reminded myself that a few bumps are part of the process and that's okay. I know that *technically* the plane barely shifted but I have a vivid imagination, so as far as my brain was concerned this plane was falling out of the sky and I needed to start getting my life in order. I went back to the process and focused on where I was going. There will be times when you feel like things aren't going to plan and you might be tempted to freak out when it gets a bit bumpy along the way, but keep coming back to the process and you'll find the direction to keep moving forward. Every now and then you may even need to turn the plane around and go back to the start because things aren't working properly, and that's okay too. Start the process again and keep moving forward.

Starting with message clarity has given you a destination and direction before you even get people on the plane. Now your focus is on getting people on board and helping them navigate the journey to where you need them to be. Here we are going to explore the *flight path structure* in more depth by highlighting five key principles that align with each stage of the journey. We will also explore some of the techniques you can use to leverage each stage of the journey to create the most impact.

BOARDING

Before you leave, *get people on the plane.*

When leaders speak below the line, they tend to adopt the mindset of *I'll speak, you listen.* As a result, people often say they feel *spoken at* rather than *communicated with.* I see this in action when a leader just starts speaking without taking time to consider whether or not people are actually listening. For them it's about getting out what they want to say rather than having a conversation.

To be blunt, this approach to communication is selfish. It's more about them than about the people they are speaking to. Great communication starts with taking time to ensure people are with you, engaged and ready to listen before you move on. But in a world where we have more information and less focus, this is becoming increasingly difficult for leaders to do.

Research conducted by Microsoft in Canada and published in 2015 suggested that since 2000 the average human attention span had decreased from 12 seconds to 8 seconds, or one second shorter than that of a goldfish. Irrespective of the research's validity (and there has been some debate on its conclusions), you don't need to look any further than yourself for evidence of this trend. Try sitting alone with a single thought for just 60 seconds and notice how often your mind wanders, or think about how often you might actually stop and read the ads in your social media feed? American economist and political scientist Herbert A. Simon explains:

> *'In an information-rich world, the wealth of information means a dearth of something else: a scarcity of whatever it is that information consumes. What information consumes is rather obvious: it consumes the attention of its recipients. Hence a wealth of information creates a poverty of attention and a need to allocate that attention efficiently among the overabundance of information sources that might consume it.'*

We have become *information rich* but *attention poor*. Every time you stand up to speak you are competing for the attention of your audience. This is the first principle to understand if you want to deliver with impact.

Principle #1: the principle of attention

If you want people to pay attention, you need to share something *remarkable*.

In November 2015 my wife and I visited the United States for the first time as adults. We arrived in New York City late at night and made our way to our accommodation in Williamsburg in Brooklyn. As you can imagine, having just come off a 20+-hour flight, neither of us could sleep because of jet lag. After hours of tossing and turning we gave up on the idea and decided to take the subway in to Manhattan to visit iconic Times Square. After all, this was 'the city that never sleeps'.

I remember getting off the subway at Grand Central Station and feeling like I was walking through a movie set. I may even have felt a bit like a celebrity for a moment in my mind. When you grow up seeing New York through a movie screen it is a surreal experience to be standing there in the midst of it all. As we threaded our way to Times Square we felt our anticipation building. Despite being deliriously tired we were excited.

Then we were there, in the epicentre of the noise and hustle, standing beside a giant LED American flag. Gazing around us, taking it all in, all I could think was…

This is overwhelming…

Maybe it was sleep deprivation, or the scale of everything, but I felt like my senses were being bombarded by the noise, the energy, the sights and sounds, the billboards and banners. Everywhere I looked I was enjoined to *buy this, have this, eat this, want this, see this*. I have to say that even though it was overwhelming, I really loved it. I just didn't know where to look next. I was locked in this continual fight for my attention.

As a leader you face this challenge every time you speak. In every room a struggle is taking place in which multiple stimuli compete for our attention. The list is long but includes:

- email and social media notifications
- temperature and room setup
- uncomfortable seating
- lighting and technical issues
- hunger
- internal thoughts and concerns.

When leaders tell me they get anxious about what people might be thinking of them as they speak, my response is to remind them that *nobody* is actually thinking about them. We are a self-absorbed species. When people walk into the room, they are thinking about themselves, how they feel, what's going on in their life or work. Your task as a leader is to pit yourself against this competition, to grab these people's attention and convince them that what you have to say is important.

How do you win the attention of people in such a contest? Answer: you do something *remarkable*.

New York is famous for the billboard bombardment of Times Square. How on earth do you promote something in the middle of such chaos? One billboard in particular caught our attention, which is hardly surprisingly as it stands eight storeys high and spans 262 metres. It is too big to fit on one block so it wraps around the corner of the building. When we were walking past it a white screen lit up like an apocalyptic vision. If you were considering advertising there, it would set you back a mere US$2.5 million a month. At the time, Google had snapped up the opportunity.

To compete successfully you must do something that silences the noise and stands out from the crowd. When I was working as a marketing consultant, I read an influential book by Seth Godin called *Purple Cow*. It's a classic business book based on the premise that if you want to stand out you need to be remarkable. If you are driving down a country road and see the usual breeds of cows it's unlikely you will stop. But drive past a purple cow and chances are you will pull over, take a photo and share it with everyone you know.

When I speak to leaders, I tell them that if you want people to pay attention you need to say this remarkable thing in the first 30 to 60 seconds. No pressure, right? I don't mean it needs to be perfect or mind blowing, but it does need to make people *want* to pay attention. It can't be like every other boring, stale presentation they are used to hearing. If you spend the first five minutes welcoming people, updating them on the minutes of your last meeting or introducing yourself, then you've blown the opportunity.

Here are five things you can do to help capture the attention and focus of people from the start.

Ask an intentional question

When we hear a question, our brain can't help but contemplate the answer.

Beginning your presentation with the right question can be a powerful way to capture your audience's attention. In *The Science of Selling: Proven Strategies to Make Your Pitch, Influence Decisions, and Close the Deal*, author David Hoffeld discusses what happens when the brain hears a question:

> '*Questions trigger a mental reflex known as "instinctive elaboration." When a question is posed, it takes over the brain's thought process. And when your brain is thinking about the answer to a question, it can't contemplate anything else.*'

Questions compel us towards thinking. When we think, we can't help but engage. The key is to ask the right kind of question, one that moves people towards our conversation and not away from it.

One of the first reservations I hear when I suggest that people start with a question is 'What if people answer?' It all depends on the size of the room and how you frame the question. If it's a small room (fewer than eight people, say), there's a greater chance someone will answer, because the setting lends itself more to a conversation than a presentation. As the room gets bigger, this response is less likely. If you pause for too long after asking the question, people are more inclined to think you are asking for a response. It's a delicate balance between allowing enough time for people to think but not enough to encourage a direct response. How you frame the question is another determinant. You could say, 'I want you to think about the answer to this question…'

Make an audacious statement

Making an audacious statement will prompt your audience to pause, reflect and consider the question *What do I think about this?*

An audacious statement is not so much about gaining agreement as about building engagement. Having people agree with what you say is less important than persuading them to think about what they believe about it. Don't misunderstand me, this isn't about creating controversy for its own sake; it's about raising expectation. Your opening line may be a statement of belief, a big idea or some data that elicits an emotional response from the audience. As with all introductions, the key is ensuring this statement or statistic causes them to think about your topic of discussion. You'll also need to be prepared to stand by your statement.

You are most likely familiar with Martin Luther King Jr's famous 'I Have a Dream' speech, but do you know how it actually began? The opening lines were:

> *'I am happy to join with you today in what will go down in history as the greatest demonstration for freedom in the history of our nation.'*

What a wildly audacious statement. But can you feel the emotion that a statement like that evokes within you? Could you put yourself in that place, hearing those words, and imagine how you might feel?

I'm not suggesting you start every presentation with 'This will be the greatest speech in the history of our company'. You might get attention, but I'm not sure it would work in your favour. It may be something as simple as 'Toxic culture has the potential to kill our company, so we're going to talk about how to protect ourselves from it' or 'We intend to double our revenue in the next 90 days'.

Share a purposeful story

Great communicators are master storytellers.

If you have ever had the privilege of speaking to a room full of people, you will understand the power of effective storytelling. As a speaker, the disposition of the room changes when you begin to share a story. People who were hitherto distracted or fidgeting begin to lean in, to focus and hang on your every word. What's more, neuroscientist Paul Zak has found, 'Character-driven stories with emotional content result in a better understanding of the key points a speaker wishes to make and enable better recall of these points weeks later'.

Effective storytelling is a skill that every leader must learn to master for several key reasons:

1. Stories are a *language* that everyone understands.
   Regardless of where in the world you travel to, people understand the power of stories. Whether it's over a glass

of wine or around a campfire or dinner table, stories are how we connect with one another. It's one of the reasons we love watching movies, reading books and opening the newspaper every day.

2. Stories help people *lean in* to you as a leader. When you share a story, especially a personal story, in those moments you break down the barriers to trust and connection and help people lean in to you as a leader. People learn a little more about who you are outside of the organisation. They see the human being behind the title.

3. Stories cause people to focus and *listen*. When you start telling a story, the atmosphere of the room changes and people actually listen. If you travel regularly with one of the major airlines you will have noticed the shift over the past few years in the pre-flight safety videos. Once stale and boring demonstrations, they have now taken on a life of their own, following the journeys of people around the world from New York to Cape Town, pairing yoga with the brace position, waterslides with escape slides. Airlines know that if they can share important information through the medium of a compelling story, the audience is more likely to stop, focus and listen.

4. Stories are how we *learn*. In preliterate times oral storytelling was how people shared experiences, knowledge and learning. Storytelling has always been humanity's way of passing wisdom from one generation to the next.

We are hardwired for stories. In *Talk Like TED*, author Carmine Gallo advises, 'If you want people to pay attention to you, wrap your idea in a story'. The story you share may be the product of personal experience or observation, or a fictional account shared as a life lesson or illustration. The key is to ensure your story supports your main message. Stories shine a spotlight on a big idea; they are not the big idea itself. I tell leaders, 'If people remember your story but forget the idea, then everyone has missed the point'.

Throw an unexpected curveball

Do something unexpected and leverage the power of surprise.

In a radio interview, self-proclaimed *surpriseologist* and author of *Surprise: Embrace the Unpredictable and Engineer the Unexpected*, Tania Luna explores the idea that when people experience a surprise the brain initiates the 'surprise sequence'.

> *'It's a strong neuro alert that tells us that something is important about this moment and we have to pay attention. Our cognitive resources are basically hijacked and pulled into the moment. That's one of the things that's really uncomfortable for some people, but also exciting for some people because your attention is completely in the moment.'*

I'm not suggesting that you jump out from behind the projector screen and startle everyone in the room, but if you find yourself in an environment with endless repetition even a simple tweak to the start of your presentation can catch people off guard and win their attention.

A couple of years ago I delivered a training day to a group of executives in the public sector. Also present in the room were a few of the HR team, one of whom regularly delivered a career planning workshop for internal employees. As you can imagine, in this type of organisation most presentations were relatively predictable. Chairs were laid out in the same format, tea and coffee were at the back, and at the front was a screen image that read 'Career Planning Workshop – Room 101.3

[organisation name – presenter name]'. One time she decided to break the script and do something different.

When people walked in, there on the screen was a beautiful picture of the night sky and a constellation of stars. Across the sky was the word 'Stargazing', and that was it. People walked in and were immediately curious about what was going to happen. She opened with a story about her fascination with astronomy. She shared what it was like the first time she looked up at the sky and thought about something so much bigger than herself. She then told the story of when she first arrived in the organisation and had her head down in her job without thinking much of the future. She drew the parallel between looking up for a moment to take in the night sky and looking up for a moment to consider where she wanted to go in her career. A year later people in other workshops I ran for the organisation still spoke of that career workshop she ran. It was a brilliant example of surprising people by throwing an unexpected curveball.

If you notice the attention of your audience is being pulled away, do something different. It could be something as simple as getting down off the stage and walking though the audience, or you could use props and visual aids to help illustrate your point.

Tap into your creative imagination

Help people see in their *mind* what they are unable to see with their eyes.

Imagination is an important tool in the hands of an effective leader and communicator. It is a powerful way to paint a picture of a desired future, to warn people of a potential danger or to share lessons from a situation that has not happened.

In 2017 I received a phone call from an HR manager who was about to speak at an important team meeting. She had been asked to highlight the importance of an updated learning management system for their employees. She needed to convince people in the room to implement a change, but she also needed a budget allocation from the leaders in the room.

We started with clarity: 'What are you trying say here?' We had to get clear on her message. She stressed to me how important up-to-date training and learning were in their sector, because they ultimately affected their ability to deliver the best service to their customers. Put simply, she wanted people to know that 'our ability to build trust with our clients is linked to our commitment to learning'. We took some time to discuss some of the ways she might open. She could have shared a personal story about the importance of learning, but we both felt like it wouldn't be enough to make people 'feel' the discomfort of the situation. We took a moment to tap into her creative imagination, and given that she was at an airport we settled on the following idea.

Imagine you are sitting on a plane about to push back from the aerobridge. You're settling down in your seat, preparing yourself for the long journey ahead. You are a little bit anxious about flying but at the same time excited to be going to your favourite holiday destination in the world (she chose Hawaii). As the noise of the engines begins to rise the pilot comes over the intercom as usual to welcome passengers on board.

'Ladies and gentlemen, this is your captain speaking. Welcome aboard this flight to Hawaii. We are set to pushback in just a few moments and will soon be on our way to Honolulu. I just need about five minutes to finish reading the instruction manual on how to fly this plane. Trust me, I'm a great pilot. I just haven't flown this type of plane before, so I just need

to learn what some of these controls actually do. I'll keep you updated, but for now sit back, relax and enjoy your trip.'

How does this scenario make you feel? Just a little anxious? Sick in your stomach? She then invited people to imagine a parallel but different scenario.

Imagine you are lying on an operating table about to go under for serious surgery. You are surrounded by nurses and in walks the anaesthesiologist, who begins to fit your mask and turn on the gas. She politely asks you to count backwards from 10 and you already feel yourself getting sleepy. As you begin counting you glance across the room and notice the chief surgeon clutching a book titled *Surgery for Dummies*.

Both scenarios caught the attention of people in the room and drew both laughter and groans. But there was more to this than amusing or shocking her audience. She followed through by communicating an important message. This was that industries and professions that depend on a high level of trust from their clients must maintain a strong commitment to learning. And that if their organisation could not commit to continuous learning, they were asking their clients to 'get on the plane' or 'get on the operating table' with blind faith in inexperienced and unskilled employees.

When she shared these stories, she told me later, she saw people in the room begin to shift and engage. They were listening to every word. Not only that, but they remembered it long after she had finished.

The first 30 to 60 seconds are vital for engaging the audience when you speak, but there is also a much bigger purpose to this. Most of the anxiety we feel when standing up to speak in public occurs in the moments *before* we have to speak and lasts only a short time into the introduction before we settle in. By taking time to think intentionally about how you will start, you build confidence in the space where you often feel incredibly vulnerable. Like a runner getting a great start off the blocks, you set yourself up for the rest of the race.

DEPARTING

Keeping people on the plane.

A boarding call gets people on the plane, but what is it that keeps them there? What stops them from turning around and walking straight back off again? It sounds like a ridiculous question, but the answer is what matters: *they haven't yet arrived where they want to be.*

For five years I lived in Docklands, just a few minutes by tram from one of Melbourne's largest train stations, Southern Cross Station. I caught the train into this station many times, because it was easier than driving, so I'd often find myself caught up in the middle of the peak-hour rush before or after work. The station is chaotic, like an ant colony full of hustling workers. When you stop and take a closer look at them, train stations are actually pretty miserable places, filled with people who, let's face it, would rather be almost anywhere else in the world than there at that moment. Everyone is stuck in transit. They aren't where they started their journey, whether that's work or home, and they haven't arrived where they want to be yet, so they are waiting or they just keep on moving.

When you have invested the time to get clarity around your message you are more convinced than anyone else in the room that what you have to say is valuable. You've got a solution to people's problems, an answer to their questions and a vision of a desired future that you want people to buy into. But just because you think it's valuable doesn't mean your audience will think the same. You can try to *take* people somewhere, but it's much more effective when people *want* to go with you. Because if you really want something it will compel you to *do* something. Think about it, if you want a holiday, you'll save for it. If you want a promotion, you'll work for it. If people want whatever it is that you are talking about, then they are more likely to listen to what you have to say.

Principle #2: the principle of tension

If you want to keep people's attention you need to make them *uncomfortable*.

When you create *tension* you make people uncomfortable, and when people are uncomfortable they want to do something about it. Tension is the discomfort we feel when we are caught between two opposing forces and want resolution (see Figure 7). The desire to change something, know something or be something compels us to take action to achieve the desired end state.

Figure 7: The resolution continuum

CURRENT STATE | ←——— TENSION ———→ | **END STATE**

If we want people to change, listen or engage in the conversation, we need to raise the level of discomfort in the current state and increase the desire for the end state. I've learned that motivation to go *there* will be low when comfort *here* is high. It makes logical sense. If I don't feel the discomfort of staying where I am, then it's unlikely I will want to listen to your reasoning for going somewhere else with you. If you don't give me a reason to listen to you, then I'm more likely to opt out part way through the journey.

A couple of years ago I read a news story about a man named Chris Hill-Scott. Chris was a founding partner in a start-up called SwiftKey, which produced a predictive text keyboard app for phones. Just a few months into the journey he became tired of the long hours and financial instability involved and made the decision to trade in his stake of the company – for a bike. If you have ever had the opportunity to launch something new or break new ground, you will understand. Without some kind of healthy tension – whether a vision, goal, desire or some type of future outcome – pulling you in the direction of your desired end state, it's easy to get caught up in the challenges that surround you and go back to comfort. Unfortunately for Chris, he made the decision to opt out of the process – to get back off the plane, metaphorically speaking. It was a decision he would later regret after his co-founders went on to sell the company to Microsoft for $346 million.

We have all experienced that discouraging feeling of looking out into a room full of people lounging back comfortably in their seats, disengaged and disconnected. Be honest, we have all probably *been* those people at some point. The posture that says 'impress me' or 'show me what you've got'. I often describe the discomfort of tension as the leader's ability to move people from the back to the front of their seat. Just as a great cliff-hanger in your favourite TV series leaves you on the edge of your seat, wanting more, creating healthy tension at the start of your presentation will cause people to sit up, pay attention and lean in to the conversation. In a 2016 *HBR* article, 'Good Presentations Need to Make People Uncomfortable', Josh Bersin recalls being first introduced to the concept of cognitive dissonance when in his high-school debating team in the 1970s. It was a relatively simple idea he would later draw on many times when preparing presentations and talks. He explains:

'If you want a group of people to adopt your point of view, start by describing some difficult or painful issue they're faced with. Maybe it's a problem they didn't realize they had, or maybe it's something they recognize as an ongoing challenge. Either way, you're forcing them to hold two contradictory things in their minds at once: either what they already believe and what you're telling them, or what they know and how they behave. That dissonance ratchets up their discomfort, which makes them want to fix it.'

You can now share your explanation of the problem and offer a possible solution, which should replace the dissonance with harmony.

In the first few moments of your presentation you have the ability to lift the level of engagement by creating healthy tension. Healthy tension is the gentle force that pulls people towards a desired end state. There are a number of ways you can do this. You can look at the current state and raise the level of pain that people feel to push them towards a desired state. You can raise curiosity, highlight the knowledge gap between the current state and the desired state, and create a tension that needs to be resolved. Or you can raise the level of expectation by creating a compelling vision of the desired end state, inspiring people towards action. Let's now look at these in more detail.

Raise the level of pain

Highlight the *problems* so people want to *change* something.

If you have a practical solution to a problem, it stands to reason that you should start by highlighting the problem. There's no point selling people a solution to a problem that they don't have or that they aren't aware they have.

One of my guilty pleasures is watching the US TV series *Shark Tank*. I like it for a couple of reasons: firstly it's dealing with much larger sums of money than the Australian series, and secondly they are so brutally honest. If you haven't watched *Shark Tank* before it is essentially a reality television program for entrepreneurs seeking venture capital. They have just a few moments to pitch their business idea to a panel of industry titans in the hope of obtaining support and funding to allow them to grow and scale their business. If you are going to pitch to the sharks, there are a few things you had better know. You need to know your numbers and have a clear idea about your finances, you need to know what problem your product solves, and you need to know who has those problems. You can be sure that if the sharks don't see how your product can solve people's problems, the conversation is going to be brutal.

A favourite episode for me was found in season 6, which aired back in 2006. Bobby Edwards and his mother, Judy, had found a solution to a problem that people experience every day; the challenge was that it was a problem nobody knew they had. Their product, called The Squatty Potty®, is a small plastic toilet stool 'designed to elevate the feet and open the colon for better elimination'. That's an elegant way of describing a plastic stool to help you poop better. It had the potential to be laughed out of the room, until they started their pitch.

I love their opening line to the sharks:

> *'There's something you are doing wrong every single day of your lives and it's adversely affecting your health.'*

They didn't start by selling a solution. They started by helping people understand the problem. This wasn't just a plastic stool to help with your stool, this was a device for better colon health. They demonstrated the health benefits of a squatting posture to enable complete elimination without straining and the dangers associated with sitting in the normal way. They started by raising the level of pain by highlighting the problem. Once the problem became clear, people wanted to change; and when you have the solution, people will sit up and listen. The product received investment and racked up over a million dollars in sales within the first 24 hours.

If you want people to listen to your solution, first take time to help people understand the problem and make people uncomfortable by raising the level of pain. I will often encourage the leaders I work with to think about and share a story that everyone in the room can relate to that illustrates the problem.

Raise the level of curiosity

Highlight the *questions* so people want to *know* something.

If you want to educate people or give people an answer, then start by helping them ask the right questions. When you ask the right question, you highlight a knowledge gap, and the tension of wanting to fill that gap in knowledge compels us to engage in the conversation.

There is a story you may have heard that has been floating around the internet for a few years. It goes like this:

> *A man's car breaks down near a monastery. He goes to the monastery, knocks on the door and asks for help. 'Do you think I could stay the night?' The monks graciously invite him in, feed him dinner, even fix his car. That night, before he falls asleep, he hears a strange sound. The next morning he asks the monks what the sound was, but they say, 'We can't tell you, because you're not a monk'. He is disappointed but thanks them and goes on his merry way.*

Some years later the same man breaks down in front of the same monastery. The monks again welcome him, feed him and fix his car. That night he hears the same strange noise he had heard years earlier. In the morning he asks again what it was, but the monks give the same response: 'We can't tell you. You're not a monk.'

The man says, 'All right, all right. But I'm dying to know. If the only way I can find out what that sound was is to become a monk, how do I become a monk?' The monks reply, 'You must travel the Earth and tell us how many blades of grass there are and the exact number of sand pebbles. When you find these numbers, you will become a monk'. The man sets about his task.

Some 54 years later he returns to the monastery. He says, 'I have done what you asked. There are 145,236,284,232 blades of grass and 231,281,219,999,129,382 sand pebbles on Earth'. The monks reply, 'Congratulations. You are now a monk'. With this they lead him to a wooden door where the head monk says, 'The sound is behind that door'.

The man reaches for the knob, but the door is locked. He says, 'That's really funny. May I have the key?' The monks give him the key, and he opens the door. Behind the wooden door is another door made of stone. The man asks for the key to the stone door. The monks give him the key, and he opens it, only to find a door made of ruby. He demands another key from the monks, who provide it. Behind that door is another door, this one made of sapphire, and so it goes until the man has passed through doors of emerald, silver, topaz and amethyst.

Finally, the monks say, 'This is the last key to the last door'.

With a deep sigh he unlocks the door, turns the knob and behind the door he is amazed to find the source of that strange sound…

But he can't tell you what it is, because you're not a monk.

It's a frustrating story of unresolved tension, but a great demonstration of the power of raising curiosity. Something inside of you yearns to know the answer to the mystery, to close the gap in knowledge.

If you want to create tension, don't just give people answers. Help them ask the right questions. Make people uncomfortable by highlighting the gap in knowledge that raises the level of curiosity in the room. When delivering a presentation, I am very intentional about taking time to think about one key question that will frame the context of my delivery and create the tension I intend to resolve at the end.

Raise the level of expectation

Highlight the *vision* so people want to *be* something.

In his book *Are You Fully Charged: The 3 Keys to Energizing Your Work and Life,* Tom Rath discusses the findings of research into the 'anticipated utility' of experiences. He explains that simply 'looking forward to an event or vacation' contributes to wellbeing and actually provides more happiness than the event itself. A team of Dutch researchers drew similar conclusions from a survey of over 1,500 adults back in 2010. They too found that the anticipation of a holiday provided more feelings of happiness than the holiday itself.

My first full-time job when I left university was a 12-month maternity leave contract in local government, where I took on the role of 'Events Development Officer'. I had spent the previous five years running and organising events, so this role was a perfect fit for that time of my life. My job focused primarily on coaching community group leaders and event managers on how to run an effective event in partnership with the local council.

I always valued my time in event management because it taught me a lot about the importance of creating a compelling vision, especially when working with volunteers. If you can't imagine a compelling vision for the future that people can aim towards and unify around, then you will struggle to keep people focused long enough to make any real progress. Whenever I was coaching event managers, I always reminded them that if they cannot give people a persuasive reason to come to the event then they won't come. They needed to show people why they would want to be there and why they should choose that event over a day at the beach.

If you want to create tension in your presentation, create a compelling vision for the future that raises the level of expectation. Paint a picture of what the future could look like if they make the decision to listen to what you have to say. Make people feel uncomfortable with the mediocrity they are currently experiencing, and inspire them to be something more. If you want people to listen, give them a reason to.

FLYING

Take time to look out the window.

When booking a flight, I am faced with the dilemma of choosing between a window seat and an aisle seat. I know there are more important things to be concerned about. The tension I experience comes down to choosing between enjoying the view or being able to stand up and walk around whenever I want to. I've started to opt for the window. There's something magical about rising over a city and bursting through the clouds into another world. The experience reminds me to keep elevating my own perspective. It challenges me to find new ways of looking at things. As we fly, the captain occasionally comes over the PA system to draw the attention of those seated on one side of the plane or the other to a city or landmark. I always feel a little envious of those seated opposite me when I'm on the wrong side.

Every time you stand up to speak, you are communicating what you see, believe, know or feel through the lens of your own perspective. A quote typically attributed Anaïs Nin reads, 'We don't see the world as it is, we see it as we are'. But that perspective may not always resonate with everyone in the room. If the way you view change is through the perspective of analytics, you may disengage those people in the room who want to hear context. If you love telling stories, you may lose people in the room who are interested only in the facts and research.

The third principle in the flight path structure focuses on communicating in a way that helps people look out of both sides of the plane.

Principle #3: the principle of perspective

If you want people to connect with your idea you need to make it *understandable*.

The idea must be coherent to more people in the room than just you. In their book *Made to Stick*, Chip and Dan Heath write about an experiment undertaken by Elizabeth Newton from Stanford University in the early 1990s. In the 'Tappers and Listeners' experiment, Newton divided her subjects into two groups. The tappers were given a list of 120 popular songs and tasked with tapping the melody to each song on the desk. The listeners had to guess the song. The key to the experiment was asking the tappers to predict what percentage of listeners they believed would guess the song correctly. The tappers predicted they would guess the song 50 per cent of the time. Of course they would, when the songs were so easy to guess.

As it turned out, just 2.5 per cent of listeners guessed the song correctly. I've personally tried this activity a number of times while speaking at conferences, tapping out the simplest, most familiar tunes, such as the national anthem or happy birthday, with similarly disappointing results.

Why couldn't the listeners guess the song? The Heath brothers attribute this to a cognitive bias called the *curse of knowledge*. When a tapper taps out a melody, they sing along to it in their head, but all the listener can hear is a series of disconnected taps. With the curse of knowledge, it becomes impossible to unlearn or know what it is like *not* to know it. The longer we have been immersed in the knowledge of something, the more difficult it becomes to remember what it was like not to have that knowledge.

In the late 1990s Christopher Chabris and Daniel Simons at Harvard University conducted an experiment testing how the brain processes visual information. In a 60-second test participants were asked to count the number of times the ball was passed between six basketball players, three in black shirts and three in white. If you haven't seen this, then I recommend you stop reading now and watch it before you read the next paragraph.

At some point in the 60-second video a person dressed in a gorilla suit walks slowly into the centre of the screen, chest beats and leaves, spending nine seconds in plain sight. You might think it would be impossible to miss a gorilla standing in full view, yet surprisingly only half of the people surveyed noticed it at all. In psychology this selective attention, where an individual fails to perceive something in plain sight, is also called *inattentional blindness* or *perceptual blindness*. It's easy to miss something obvious when you're not intentionally looking for it or when you have become familiar with it over time.

In a former job I was asked to oversee a building renovation project. We were on a tight schedule, needing to complete the work in just seven days. Part of the project included updating the colour scheme of the walls to match the new branding. After a week of long days and nights we completed the project just in time for the opening the following week. As I walked through with the manager we stopped and looked at a set of unpainted partitions that had somehow been overlooked. He looked at me and said, 'We need to get these painted as soon as possible or they will stay like this forever.' I laughed and added it to the list of things that needed to be done.

Three years later those doors were still the original colour. What was worse, nobody even noticed (not even me). For the first few weeks people pointed them out and said we should do something about it. Eventually people became accustomed to the colour, and soon people didn't even notice. Three years later someone walked into the building and pointed out the colour of the doors – a fresh set of eyes brought a new perspective – and we had the doors painted immediately.

I see the curse of knowledge and inattentional blindness at work right across the leadership space. Immersed in the strategic plan, a leader makes the assumption that everyone knows what the strategic goals are. A technical expert spends all their time immersed in a product and can't understand why some people's eyes glaze over in the face of technical jargon.

I have trained leaders to think about each idea they share through four different lenses (see Figure 8). Two of these communicate using a perspective that leans towards *left brainers*, who love analytical, logical and concrete thinking; the other two favour *right brainers*, who love creative, abstract and emotive thinking.

Figure 8: The lenses of understanding

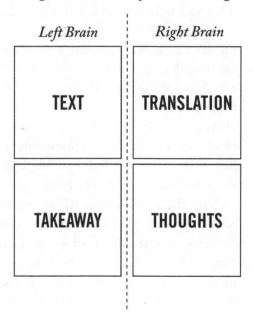

Text

The first lens focuses directly on the subject matter or key piece of information. It gives a part of the context for the idea you want to share. Concrete and often analytical, it may comprise compelling data, research findings, a case study, a historical account, or a process or model. In every room you walk into there will people who are (perhaps unconsciously) waiting for evidence to support what you say. This is about finding that evidence, demonstrating to these people that you have done the work and understand your subject.

Translation

How can you share your key text or information in a new way to make it equally comprehensible to people who think differently?

What picture might help people visualise the data? Do you have a personal story to illustrate the research findings? If you are talking about a historical account, what would that look like today?

Recently I spoke at a conference alongside a former Australian Olympic athlete. As he shared some of his own personal journey, he mentioned that one of the events he participated in was the long jump. He told us that the world record for long jump was 8.9 metres. I looked across the room when he said those words and a handful of people nodded, but most didn't seem impressed. I think he knew in that moment that people weren't grasping this idea. They heard the 'text', but it wasn't really resonating in the way he hoped. So he stepped down off the stage and called for a volunteer. A woman stood up and he walked her to the right side of the room. 'Wait here,' he said. 'I'm not going to ask you to jump, but I need you to help me out!' He then paced out roughly 8.95 metres across the room. The platform he was speaking from was about 3 metres wide, so you can imagine the look on people's faces as he took nine long strides across the room. For the athlete 8.95 metres was part of his curse of knowledge. Recognising this, he effectively translated that information in a way that connected with everyone in the room.

Thoughts

Why are you sharing this information? This lens focuses on unpacking your personal thoughts and reflections on the subject matter. People don't just want to know what others have said; they want to know what you think. There's a reason you have been given the opportunity to speak on this topic, and this is your opportunity to give it. They want to know how this can be applied in their context. Is this information useful or not? What should they think, feel or do about what you have shared?

Takeaway

Now you have given people your thoughts, what do you want people to do with the information? Once your message is distilled to its essentials, what can people actually take away and use from what you have shared? Everything you share should build towards practical application. What would you like people to do when they walk away with the information you have given them?

LANDING

A smooth touchdown. Have you ever worked so hard and been so close to achieving something, only to miss out at the last moment? It's a horrible feeling. Spare a thought for Japanese snowboarder Reira Iwabuchi, who missed out on becoming the youngest ever female Japanese medallist at the 2018 Winter Olympics. A news article in *The Japan Times* recounted:

> 'At 16 years and two months, Iwabuchi would have rewritten the record set by figure skater Mao Asada at 19 years, five months at the 2010 Vancouver Olympics had she made it to the podium. After the first two runs, Iwabuchi was 10 points behind third place and fellow 16-year-old Zoi Sadowski-Synnott of New Zealand, who fell on her third run to give Iwabuchi a shot at the podium. But Iwabuchi botched her landing, throwing Sadowski-Synnott a lifeline. Iwabuchi finished with 147.50 points after a 79.75 in the first run and 67.75 in the second.'

As I read Reira's story, I thought about how much work she would have put in to prepare for the Games, the physical toll it would have taken on her body, and every obstacle she would have needed to overcome along the way. To miss because she wasn't able to *stick the landing* would have been devastating. Coming fourth at an Olympics is something to be incredibly proud of, but like every great athlete she was obviously striving for a medal.

Over the years I have watched many presentations, keynotes and talks. What I have noticed about great communicators is that they know how to stick the landing. They don't just know how to open and deliver a great presentation; they know how to end well. It is glaringly obvious when a person hasn't put enough thought into how they will end.

It usually means:

- an abrupt ending (that's all I have to say, folks)

- an abuse of time (with everyone wondering if it will ever end)

- an awkward transition (with everyone wondering if that *was* the end).

We often rehearse, critique and analyse how we mean to start. But it's also crucial to think through how we will end. Because nobody likes a bumpy landing. As you bring your presentation in to land you need to think about creating *resolution* for people. If you have created tension in the mind of your audience, then you need to resolve that tension or risk frustrating them. If you have raised a question, you need to offer an answer. If you have highlighted a problem, you need to be ready with a solution. If you have given people half of a story, you need to offer an ending.

Principle #4: the principle of resolution

If you want people to remember, then you need to make it *memorable*.

I don't really have favourites when it comes to this process, but if I did this would be it. I cannot overemphasise the importance of having one clear memorable message that brings resolution to your delivery.

In the earlier mentioned podcast with Don Miller from *StoryBrand*, Andy Stanley discussed how he prepared to speak at President Obama's inauguration. At one point he observed, 'Memorable is portable', by which he meant that if we can get people to remember our message it is more likely that people will take it with them and incorporate it into their life and work.

I spoke at a conference back in 2017 about the importance of messaging for leaders. Afterwards we had a short break for morning tea and a man asked me a seemingly simple question: 'What was Hillary Clinton's presidential campaign slogan?' I paused for a moment to think. 'I don't know,' I admitted. He then posed another question: 'What was Trump's?' I laughed, because despite the fact that I didn't follow politics closely, even I knew the answer to that question. 'Make America Great Again,' I replied confidently. He smiled and kept walking, and I understood the point he was making.

I've since heard a number of people use that example with other presidents such as Obama. I have learned over time that if you want people to remember something, *you* have to make it memorable. If people can't remember what you said, it isn't that they have a retention issue; it's that you have a communication issue. In her book *Powerful: Building a Culture of Freedom and Responsibility*, Patty McCord suggests that people aren't 'too stupid to listen'; rather, 'you made it too complicated to understand'. Again, I'm not suggesting that it was one message that won an election, but you cannot deny the value of an impactful message.

So what makes a great message? An impacting message should be *easy to remember* and *hard to forget*.

As you bring resolution to your delivery you need to leave people with one big idea. This idea should be *succinct* enough that people remember it while being *stimulating* enough that it is hard for them to forget. Think of it like a song that gets stuck in your head. You want everyone in the room to walk away from your delivery singing your tune.

Think of some simple messages and ideas that stick with us. Take a look at these:

> *Treat others as you want to be treated.*
>
> *If it's not broken, don't fix it.*
>
> *Two wrongs don't make a right.*
>
> *Hope for the best, but prepare for the worst.*
>
> *Actions speak louder than words.*
>
> *One person's trash is another person's treasure.*
>
> *Familiarity breeds contempt.*

You could readily make a list of your own. Every leader needs to be able to construct a clear message that connects in three distinct ways:

Logically

Does your message make people *think*?

Your message should make sense in itself and cause people to think about it in a positive way. If it's too complex to understand, people are less likely to think about it and more likely to discard it. As with every great song that gets stuck in your head, you should be able to remember the words and make sense of what you are singing. Your message should also have a single focus. Don't try to add too many ideas into one message or it's likely people won't remember any of them.

If you want people to remember and think about your message, then it makes sense that it be succinct. Psychological tests suggest that at any one time the average person is able to recall (or hold in their working memory) around seven separate objects or ideas, plus or minus two. I'm not suggesting that your message must be no longer than nine words, though if you could manage that you would probably be doing yourself a favour!

One of the techniques I have found most valuable in developing messaging is around the concept of light and shade or contrast. By using words or phrases that contrast with each other, people need to remember only the first half of the expression to recall the second. Look back at some of the light and shade in the messages listed above:

others – you
broken – fix
wrongs – right
best – worst
actions – words
trash – treasure
familiarity – contempt

I use this technique regularly when writing for social media. For example, I recently read an article about how condescension is one of the least tolerated behaviours in a manager. My thought was, *If you want people to respect you and look up to you as a leader, you need to treat them with respect and avoid condescending communication.* Not very memorable, is it? So I distilled it and used a contrasting approach, eventually landing on this:

It's hard to look up to a leader who always speaks down to you.

This is something people are surely more likely to think about than the longer form.

Other examples of messages I have used in the past include:

Silence speaks volumes.

Strong teams aren't built with weak communication.

I have included numerous examples of succinct messaging throughout this book.

Emotionally

Does your message make people *feel*?

Like every great song, your message should evoke a response at an emotional level. People should be able to hear it and think about it but also *feel* something as they hear or read the words. Does your message have a rhythm and flow off the tongue easily? Language matters. What words have you chosen to communicate your idea? Like an artist working with a palette, choose the words that fit best with one another and create a flow.

Looking back at the Trump administration's main message for the 2016 campaign, 'Make America Great Again', the words were carefully chosen to trigger an emotional response. It should be said that the message was not a new one. (Ronald Reagan kicked off his 1980 presidential campaign with the slogan 'Let's make America great again'.) But take a look at the emotion invested in each of these four words in isolation:

Make – suggesting action, progress and effort

America – our home, nation and people, invoking patriotism

Great – above average, exceptional

Again – aspirational, a desire to bring back former glory

This message isn't just memorable; each word carries emotional weight, and something that connects with us on an emotional level is more likely to stay with us.

An ideal is a message that crosses cultures, philosophies and religions. Think about *Treat others as you want to be treated*. It could have been simplified to *Treat others well*, but by choosing to incorporate the words that make us reflect on how we would like to be treated, the expression becomes exponentially more potent. It makes people *feel* something and not just think something.

Aspirationally

Does your message make people *act*?

Great messages have an aspirational quality to them. They don't just make a person think or feel; they inspire them to take action. When they hear, think and feel, they'll want to walk away and do. *Make America great again* creates the aspiration of getting on with the job. *Treat others as you want to be treated* is something you can start doing today but spend the rest of your life striving to get better at. *Actions speak louder than words*, too, is a challenge you can adopt today and spend your whole life living by.

- If you can craft a message that makes people think and feel, it is more likely it will be *catchy*.

- If you can craft a message that makes people feel and do, it is more likely to be *compelling*.

- If you can craft a message that makes people think and do, it is more likely to be *constructive*.

As you bring your presentation in to land, and bring *resolution* to the tension you have created, you should be able to answer this question:

Question 1: What then?

Posing this question gives people *confirmation* and reduces the chances of misinterpretation.

After all is said and done, what then is the 'big idea' behind this? What is the 'one thing' you want people to walk away with? What is the simple message you set out to communicate? Boil everything you have spoken about down to a single sentence. This is the answer people will give when asked, 'What did they talk about?' Before you finish you must you confirm with your audience the message you have tried to communicate.

DISEMBARKING

Get people off the plane.

The goal is not just to get people *to* somewhere, but to help them *do* something. I often tell the people I coach that our aim is not just to *inform* but to *transform* people's thinking and behaviour. If as a leader your goal is to influence, lead and mobilise the people you are speaking to, then you must be able to do more than inspire people with an impacting message. You must mobilise people towards practically applying it.

I spent seven years of my life as a church minister and was fortunate to have many opportunities to speak regularly on a Sunday alongside some of the most outstanding communicators I know. Let's be honest, it's easy to get people to show up and hear you speak when you're paying them, and a completely different situation when they decide to show up on their day off. Whenever we hosted training for new and upcoming speakers there was one thought you could be sure would show up: 'Every time you speak, make sure that Sunday speaks to Monday.'

This was an idea that was so ingrained in the culture of our leadership team that anyone could recite it. It was a benchmark for every speaker who wanted to make sure that what they spoke about on Sunday in a *spiritual* context was made relevant and applicable for people to take into their real-life context on Monday. Regardless of their personal beliefs or opinions about spirituality, I think this lesson is invaluable for leaders who have to communicate.

Is what you are saying *now* speaking to what people need to do *next*? I don't just mean is this speaking to what people want to do long term, but does it give people something they can do right now? Does it compel people to take action right away?

Principle #5: the principle of action

If you want people to do something with what you share, you need to make the next step *accessible*.

In the New York City office for Weight Watchers, an organisation committed to helping people build healthy habits, staff are invited to pick up a piece of fruit when they arrive at work. This isn't surprising given the nature of the organisation. It's also not surprising how the offering changes if you arrive late. Early arrivals will find bananas among other fruit. If you arrive late it's likely you'll find only oranges. It isn't because the managers are punishing the latecomers but rather that bananas tend to go first while oranges hang around in the bowl. Tania Luna and Jordan Cohen call this the *Banana Principle*. They found that it could be explained in part by how much effort people are willing to put into eating their fruit. Bananas are easier to eat, while oranges can be a bit more messy. I once asked a conference room why they thought bananas were the first to go and one quick-witted joker called out, 'Because they are more a-peeling'. I almost instantly regret putting that line in this book. The goal of change should be to make it as accessible as possible for people to act. You can read about the banana principle in the *HBR* article titled 'To Get People to Change, Make Change Easy'.

Do you remember playing with a hose out on the driveway as a child? There was nothing like being able to jump around under the hose on a hot day to cool down in summer. I remember competing with my siblings over whose water trail would run down the driveway to the road first. Not the most exciting activity you could imagine, but this was before Netflix! What I didn't understand then was the principle of the path of least resistance. When the water hit an obstruction it found the easiest path around it and kept moving forward. People are the same, we all favour the path of least resistance. Recognising this, if you want people to take action you need to make that action as unobstructed as possible. What do you want people to know? What do you want people to do? What do you want people to be? Now how can you provide a pathway of least resistance for them to take action right away?

If you have ever been on a weight loss journey you will relate to the stated ambition 'I want to lose __ kilos'. It's usually how our fitness goal starts, and most likely we give voice to our resolution just after a delicious Christmas lunch. We look at the end point and are inspired by the challenge, maybe even put up a vision board to that effect. But when the alarm goes off at 6 o'clock the next morning we are faced with the reality of achieving that goal. *I now have to get up early and exercise, join a gym, eat better, buy new shoes and workout clothes.* That shining goal now seems so far out of reach that it fizzles out into nothing. We need an aspirational goal, but it must be partnered with an accessible next step.

If the principle of resolution depends on asking 'What then?', the principle of action depends on asking:

Question #2: What if?

This gives people *aspiration*.

What would it look like if the people you spoke to actually did what you were asking them to do? How would their life be better? How would their business or organisation be better? What would it look like if everyone did it? How would their world and the world be a better place? If we can paint this picture well for people, they will have the motivation they need to start.

Question #3: What next?

This gives people *application*.

What's the practical next step from here? How can people walk away and take immediate action? It's valuable to give people multiple strategies for how they can apply the challenge you have presented them with, but ask them to choose something to take action on now. Inspiring people is great; helping them change is better.

I once asked someone for advice about my weight loss journey and much to my surprise he didn't just tell me to lose 20 kilos. He asked me what life would look like if I was healthier. He wanted me to picture a future in which my action was successful. Then he asked me what I would do now. I said, 'I'll work out every day,' thinking that was the right response. He said, 'Okay, what will you do next?' I said, 'I guess I should go to the gym?' Much to my surprise he said, 'Yes, great. But what will you do next?' I laughed and said, 'I guess I'd better join a gym.' Almost impatiently he said, 'Yes you should, but what will you do next?' I said, 'I'll give them a call and make an appointment'. 'Great idea!' He smiled and sent me on my way. Yes, I wanted to lose 20 kg, but my first step was to call the gym. Of course I could do that. It was easy. From there I built the momentum of a successful next step to take the one after.

Whenever I mentor leaders who have to deliver a message to their team or executive, I ask them, 'What can people do next with what you have delivered to them?' The answer almost always starts vague and somewhere a long way off in the future. It sounds something like 'I want my team to collaborate more' or 'I want the board to implement a new policy'.

I once worked with a leadership team who said they wanted to break down silos in their teams. Talk about an ambitious goal! I asked them what people could do next? Eventually we landed on a simple idea: each team member should find one person on another team and ask them, 'What do you love about your work?' Start small, but start now.

If your message is about increasing buy-in on a project, your next step may be as simple as 'I will send you a calendar invite to a forum – all I need you to do is accept it'. It's easier to turn a moving car than a stationary one, so get the wheels moving.

The flight path process is all about helping people go on a journey from where they are to where we need them to be, to take away one key message and do something as a result. The goal of every leader is not to persuade people to listen, but to have them change.

When preparing to speak, this structure can usually fit on an A4 page. I have delivered a 90-minute presentation from just one such framework, intentionally completed.

CHAPTER 8
A FEW MORE THINGS TO CONSIDER

TO CONNECT, LEARN THE LANGUAGE

As leaders we will always struggle to lead the room if we cannot learn to speak the language of the room.

I have recounted how Cassandra and I celebrated our fifth wedding anniversary in 2013 by travelling to Europe to run the Marathon de Paris. The six months leading into the race were physically gruelling. Day after day we were out on the road. Our legs were like rubber, we were exhausted but we knew we needed to put in the work if we were going to finish. When we finally landed in Paris and began to navigate public transport from the airport to the hotel, it occurred to us that we'd omitted something important. In all our physical preparation and training, we hadn't put any effort into learning the French language.

For the first time we were in a foreign country and speaking to people who couldn't understand what we were saying. We just wanted to know where to go, but of course everyone wanted to tell us in French. We couldn't *connect*.

It was a valuable lesson.

If you want to connect, you need to learn the language. In your workplace and teams you cannot lead or connect if you haven't taken time to learn and speak in a way that resonates with those you lead. When you have the opportunity to speak, you should practise and prepare well. But all the practice and preparation in the world is meaningless if you can't connect your content with the people in the room.

In my training workshops, I distinguish between the different groups of people you will be speaking to at any given time (see Figure 9) and explore how your language needs to adapt based on the context of the room.

Figure 9: Identifying audience groups

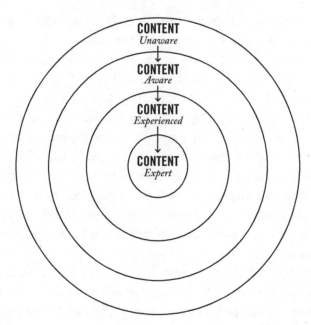

The four audience groups I identify are:

1. **The content unaware.** They have no frame of reference for the content you are delivering, so the language used must be simple and broad (e.g. an IT specialist speaking at an 'Introduction to Computing' course).

2. **The content aware.** They have limited understanding of the content but may have some first-hand experience, so the language used will be simple but can be more detailed on the topic (e.g. an IT specialist speaking at an all-staff meeting to launch the new helpdesk system).

3. **The content experienced.** They have a broad understanding of the content coupled with first-hand experience, so the language used can be more complex and detailed (e.g. an IT specialist speaking at an internal IT offsite meeting).

4. **The content experts.** They have extensive knowledge and experience of the content being discussed. The language used can therefore be highly complex, and the content must create deeper understanding for the audience (e.g. an IT specialist speaking at an IT leaders' conference on cloud-based platforms).

Next time you speak, take a moment to reflect on who will be in the room. Where would they sit in this model? Then reflect on the type of language you should use in your presentation. You must speak at the level of your audience's understanding.

FOUR QUESTIONS PEOPLE ASK EVERY TIME YOU SPEAK

I'm not a mind reader, but as someone who has sat through countless presentations and conferences, I can share with you four big questions I ask every time I hear someone speak. If you are a leader or communicator who wants to better connect with your audience, they are questions worth considering.

Question #1: Do you believe this?

This question is about *energy*.

When you speak, people want to know that you stand by your words. They won't believe you if you don't. There is something contagious about the passion and energy a person radiates when they are convinced of their content and message. It is also glaringly obvious when a person is delivering a message they don't personally believe in. Passion isn't just in volume, but in value. You don't need to be loud; you just need to care. There are many friends I would describe as passionate and yet they are anything but charismatic extroverts.

Build conviction. Get passionate about your message. Passion is seen not in *volume* so much as *value*. To become passionate about what you do, invest the time and effort into understanding deeply why your message is valuable to you and to those you share it with.

Question #2: Do I believe you?

This question is about *authenticity*.

An audience would rather engage with someone who is raw and authentic than with someone who is polished and fake. An audience will forgive you for tripping over a few words, but they won't forgive someone they perceive as bogus. Trust is the foundation for connecting your message.

Avoid comparison. Ultimately people want to connect with you, but they can't do that if you're trying to be someone else. The best pathway to authenticity is being comfortable in your own skin. Find how you communicate most naturally, own it, then keep growing.

Question #3: Do you care about me?

This question is about *generosity*.

Is your content seeking or serving? Are you sharing this information because you believe it will benefit those who are listening, or is your sole intention to seek something from them? As the popular saying goes, people don't care how much you know until they know how much you care.

Deliver value. Whether it is a sales pitch, a department update or a change process, focus on adding value first, before asking for anything in return. Put simply, always seek to give more than you take.

Question #4: Do you understand me?

This question is about *empathy*.

People want to know you've done the work to understand them. This means answering the 'what's in it for me' question before you enter the room. Empathy has been described as the ability to walk in someone's shoes and see things from their perspective. It's also the ability to find the connection between the content or message you deliver and the challenges people face.

Show understanding. Show people you have done the work required to determine how your big idea is relevant to the key challenge they face.

TO SLIDE OR NOT TO SLIDE IS NOT THE QUESTION

'Should I use slides when I present or not?' The answer to that question depends a great deal on which 'expert' you ask. You don't have to dig too deep to find an abundance of opposing perspectives on this topic. But I'm not here to tell you what to do.

I have seen great communicators who choose to use slides and others who choose not to. Both have been impacting and memorable.

I'm not here to teach you how to create great slides either. There is a wealth of resources you can access to help you do that brilliantly. I'm here to provoke your thinking.

Before you click 'Insert new slide', here are four questions to consider.

Question #1: Who does this serve?

This is a question about *benefit*.

Who ultimately benefits from this slide, you or the audience? (Hint: the answer should not be you.)

One of the biggest criticisms of presentation software is that it is used by many presenters as a crutch. That's a harsh but fair criticism. Too often when I ask people *why* they have a slide deck, the response sounds something like 'So I can remember what I'm there to say'. I have grave concerns about an audience remembering what you have said if you can't remember it yourself.

Question #2: What am I trying to say?

This is a question about *message*.

Great messaging is more than just saying something; it's about having something valuable to say.

You don't get a second chance to make a first impression. What is the first thing people think when they see this slide? What is the *one big idea* you are trying to communicate? You have just a few seconds to get your message across – is this slide doing so effectively? Does what people are seeing align with what they are hearing?

Communication specialist Alex Rister explains it like this:

> *'Your slide should pass the three-second rule of glance media. Consider billboard advertising. If an automobile driver can't process that billboard in three seconds, he or she (a) won't*

digest or act on the advertisement and (b) will probably wreck the car trying to read more than three seconds of information. Think of your audience as those drivers. If it takes them more than three seconds to process your slide, you're wrecking their chances of processing and acting on the material you're presenting.'

Question #3: Where do I want people to look?

This is a question about *focus*.

People will read a slide, or they will listen to you. They won't do both.

I've read and heard rules about how much text can be included on a slide. Personally, I hold to the 'less is more' argument and prefer to use imagery that supports my key message rather than lots of text. But every now and then I want people to read a quotation or to visualise a written concept. I have found this is okay so long as I remain aware of the audience's focus.

When you have a quote or block of text coming up that you want people to read, be sure to frame the moment. Try something like 'Take a moment to read the quote in this slide...' and pause to give them time to do so before you continue.

Question #4: How else could this be shared?

This is a question about *purpose*.

Does this need to be on a slide? Is there another way this information could be communicated?

Rather than filling up a slide with words and definitions, could they be printed on a card and handed out to people as they leave? Rather than displaying a detailed graph, could you present just the key data you are discussing? Could you send a document with additional information for participants to pre-read before the presentation?

Each slide's primary purpose is to support and reinforce the presenter's key message.

TIMEKEEPING MATTERS

Nance Duarte, author of *slide:ology: The Art and Science of Presentation Design*, observes, 'People in your audience will never scold you for ending early, but they certainly will for ending late'.

Don't mistake the brevity of this point to mean I think it's unimportant. It is crucial. When you deliver, whether at a town hall, a conference or a team meeting, be sure that you honour the time you are given. Arriving and/or finishing late is disrespectful both to the person organising the event and to your audience. People may forget what you said but they will never forget how you made them late for their next appointment!

PART 3
DEVELOPING

Great communicators obsess about *developing*. Because if you don't grow, you won't last. Our world is in a constant state of change, and leaders need to know how to grow with and adapt to the change.

If you want to see how quickly trends come and go, I recommend volunteering in a high school. In one of my earlier roles I had the opportunity to spend half a day a week mentoring students at a local high school. My time there was always full of surprises. I was never really sure what I was going to be facing when I showed up at the school office. I would take students who were going through some challenges at school and we would sit in the courtyard and talk. It's amazing what you learn when you just stop and let them speak.

I was always fascinated by how quickly the trends seemed to come and go. First kids were planking, then tebowing, doing the Harlem shake, filming the ice bucket challenge then the cinnamon challenge, it was nearly impossible to keep up. I would pick up a conversation after being away for a week, only to be met with 'Nobody's doing *that* anymore, Shane'.

But it isn't just high-school students who are experiencing constant change. Look at some of the world's leading businesses that failed to grow and adapt and suffered the consequences. Do you remember Kodak, MySpace, Nokia, Toys 'R' Us? What happened to Blockbuster?

When I was growing up Blockbuster was synonymous with Friday night. I remember going to the store to pick out movies with my date; it was the nineties version of Netflix and Chill. Kids today will never know the pain we felt going to the video store to get the latest release, to find that empty box indicating that someone had beaten us to it. Or the satisfaction of tipping seven video boxes into the back of the car when they had a weekly special running. While Blockbuster grew and adapted successfully to the shift from VHS to DVD and even Blu-Ray, they failed to innovate when Netflix began to ship-on-demand and then to stream. A business that once boasted more than 80,000 employees globally is now a relic of the past and a stark reminder of the importance for companies of constant innovation.

Where there is health, there is growth, and healthy leaders commit to growth and development. Developing is the obsession that sits at the intersection of *how* you deliver in the most impactful way and how you become the best version of *who* you are. I have found these two principles to be intrinsically linked. If you become the best version of you and feel confident in who you are, you will get better at how you deliver. At the same time, being open and receptive to external feedback and making progress in how you deliver will help you become a better version of who you already are.

I'm talking about a commitment to continual progress, not perfection. Thomas Curran and Andrew Hill wrote on the dangers of perfection in their 2018 *HBR* article titled 'Perfectionism Is Increasing, and That's Not Good News':

> *'Perfection is an impossible goal. Those who become preoccupied with it inevitably set themselves up for failure and psychological turmoil. They become obsessed with winning the validation of others and demonstrating their worth through flawless performance after flawless performance. They ruminate chronically about their imperfections, brood over what could have been or should have been, and experience considerable anxiety and even shame and guilt about their perceived inadequacies and unworthiness.'*

Practice makes perfect, the saying goes. When I work with clients, I tell them that *practice makes progress*, and that is enough.

A focus on *developing* is not an obsessive quest for perfection, but rather a mindset of continual growth and progress.

Sarah Caldwell, an American opera conductor, once said, 'Learn everything you can, any time you can, from anyone you can – there will always come a time when you will be grateful you did.' I couldn't agree more.

When it comes to leadership development, I think it's possible to fast-track growth through two key 'abilities'.

I am privileged to work in a diverse range of corporate organisations and environments, helping leaders and teams to communicate more effectively. So when the opportunity to work with a group of high-school student leaders presented itself I thought it would be a fun change of scenery. During a workshop with the students I witnessed something extremely powerful. What they did might seem simple, but it completely changed the atmosphere of the room.

Early in the day we were exploring the anxiety people experience before public speaking. I posed a simple question 'What are you afraid of?' and asked the students to write their answer on a Post-it® note and stick it on the window.

I wasn't ready for what happened next. Right away students began writing note after note detailing their fears. The conversation that followed was exhilarating. The energy in the room was palpable. These students didn't care about what others were thinking. They weren't trying to protect their ego or career. They weren't worried about missing out on a promotion. Not only were they brutally honest about their challenges, but they were ready to learn and discover ways to overcome them.

And that's what we did together.

That day I saw in action how leadership growth can be fast-tracked at the intersection of two key 'abilities', *vulnerability* and *teachability*. In this context *vulnerability* is the courage to speak up and let our walls down. By *teachability* I mean the willingness to change by being self-aware enough to acknowledge our limitations and humble enough to allow others to help. I have found this intersection to be a powerful place.

If we are unwilling to change and refuse to acknowledge this to others, we *stunt* our growth. If we are willing to change but refuse to speak up and ask for help, we *delay* our growth. If we are willing to ask for help but refuse to change, we only hurt ourselves and restrict our growth. If, on the other hand, we have the courage to speak up and let people know we need help and are willing to learn and change, we *accelerate* our growth.

Here are three ways I have seen teachability and vulnerability fast-track growth (also see Figure 10 overleaf):

1. **Fast-tracked connection.** We admire strength, but we connect through vulnerability. We learn that we are not alone in our struggles, and we are more willing to reach out to those around us for help.

2. **Fast-tracked learning.** The faster we can acknowledge our limitations and recognise there are things we do not know, the faster we can learn and grow.

3. **Fast-tracked collaboration.** We become increasingly aware of our need of others and of the power of partnership and collaboration.

To fast-track and accelerate our leadership growth, we need to be vulnerable enough to speak up when we need help and teachable enough to receive help when it's offered.

Figure 10: How teachability and vulnerability fast-track growth

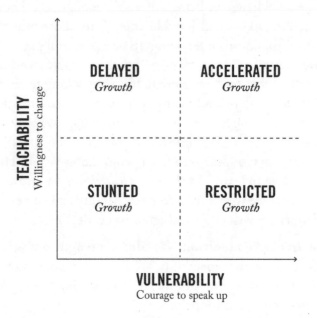

In the following chapters, I will explore four practices I believe every leader needs to commit to getting better at if they want to continue to develop as a leader and as a communicator:

1. **Thinking** – leading the brain

2. **Investing** – sharpening your skills

3. **Asking** – seeking out feedback

4. **Failing** – dealing with disappointment.

There are many others we could explore, but from my own experience I have seen the impact of great results when I gain control over my thinking, keep sharpening my skills, receive and apply consistent feedback, and handle and learn from failure.

CHAPTER 9
GET BETTER AT THINKING

If you want to lead the room, you first need to be able to lead your brain.

Last December I was reading through the usual end-of-year posts on LinkedIn, wishing everyone a Merry Christmas and reflecting on the year that had been. Someone had posted a status that was gaining a lot of traction. They asked the question, 'What is your best advice in 5 words or less?' The answers were incredibly diverse; at the time of writing over 450 people had offered their words of wisdom. This post caught my attention because one of my connections, Dr Amy Silver, a clinical psychologist, had contributed these five simple words.

'Get control over your thoughts.'

I wanted to reach through the screen and push this post to the top and delete all the others. Not because the others were wrong or unhelpful – there were some brilliant thoughts – but because I so wholeheartedly agreed with Amy. When it comes to growth and development, I believe that the ability to gain control over your thoughts and develop better thinking is a leader's most potent secret weapon.

Whenever I work with people who know they need to communicate more from a platform, I am met with the same objections:

- 'It's not really my thing.'
- 'I'm not great at public speaking.'
- 'I'd rather give someone else a go.'

Then the usual fears around public speaking are voiced:

- What if people laugh at me?
- What if I go blank, forget what to say or look stupid?
- What if I'm asked a question and I don't know the answer and look like an idiot?
- What if the technology fails and I don't know what to do?
- What if people think I'm no good at my job or even as a person?
- What if I lose my credibility?

Those last two may have cut a little deep, but if you're human and anything like the hundreds of people I have worked with, then you are sure to recognise one or two of these thoughts. Every time I run a workshop I ask people to write down their biggest fears, share and discuss them at their table, and bring one unique fear out to the front. In all of the workshops I have run I have never seen a comment that stops me and makes me say, 'Wow, I've never heard that before'. Deep down we all have the same fears; we just don't usually talk about them.

I have found that most of our challenges with confidence around public speaking come back to dysfunctional thinking. Learning to control and get better at our thinking changes how we feel about speaking. What I'm sharing here isn't new. You can learn about dysfunctional thinking from almost any book on cognitive behavioural therapy (CBT). But here I want to look at it specifically in relation to the fear of presenting.

To get control over your thinking my advice to the people I work with can be summed up in just three words: *recognise, reframe, refocus.*

RECOGNISE

Notice your thoughts.

Have you noticed that before every epic movie battle scene, on the cusp of combat, one leader steps or rides out in front of the army to rally the troops, whether it's William Wallace in *Braveheart*, Maximus in *Gladiator* or Coach Bombay in *The Mighty Ducks*. There is always a moment right before the battle when the troops need inspiration. It doesn't happen in the midst of the fighting out on the field; it's in those few moments before battle. Why? Because that's the moment when your imagination runs wild and your thoughts of disaster plague you. Once you're in the fight, your training takes over and the adrenalin kicks in. If the leader can lead their thinking just long enough for this training to kick in, then they will run head-on into the battle.

Most of the challenges with public speaking are the same. Once you start speaking and get into your presentation, your preparation and training kicks in. The challenge is in those few vulnerable moments before you walk on stage or as someone introduces you. That's when you need to recognise the dangers of dysfunctional thinking.

There are a few reasons why we experience dysfunctional thoughts.

Our desire for belonging

Throughout human history we have survived and thrived through collaboration and community. If banished from your tribe, you had to fend for yourself and lose the security of the group, and your chances of survival were greatly reduced. It's scarcely surprising, then, that if you sense any type of threat to belonging or fitting in among your peers or community, then you would instinctively try to avoid the threat. Why put yourself in a position where you might risk banishment? If you see no way out, you can be sure your brain will be warning you that you'd better not stuff this up.

But think about it. When was the last time you stumbled over the words in your presentation and found yourself fired from your job, living on the streets and fending for yourself, having been isolated from your community?

Negative past experiences

One of my most traumatic public speaking experiences happened when I was still in high school. We had been assigned to speak for just four minutes on a text that had influenced our life in some way. I started well and had people engaged throughout the presentation. Everything was running smoothly, until I had to bring this plane in to land. *How do I finish? How do I end this thing?* As I approached the runway I aborted the landing and decided to circle the airport one more time, reiterating some of my main points and ideas. Nine minutes into a four-minute presentation I took another shot at the landing, only to pull out again. Fourteen minutes passed, then sixteen minutes. At the nineteen-minute mark my teacher walked up to the front where I was standing, gently placed his hand on my shoulder and whispered, 'I think it's time to wrap up'. I said, 'Thank you for your time', and took the walk of shame back to my desk, waiting for the ground to swallow me up. One person who clearly felt empathy gave a single clap. Not multiple, just one. The room was silent, and the bell rang for lunch. 'We will continue presentations tomorrow,' our teacher announced as we left the room, and I got out of there as fast as I could.

For a long time I carried the weight of this negative experience into future opportunities. Every time someone would ask me to speak, I flashed back to that fiasco and turned down the opportunity. Why would I want to put myself through that again?

Just because you've had a negative experience once, does that mean you should give up? Think about it for a moment. If that theory was logical, then you'd probably never have learned to walk, ride a bike or shop at Aldi. Get control over the thoughts that lead you to believe that because that's how it *has been* it's the way it always *will be*.

Unhelpful beliefs

Just because everyone's doing it doesn't mean you have to. For a long time, people have held on to the belief that public speaking is an inherently stressful activity. Jerry Seinfeld once joked that the fear of public speaking ranks higher than the fear of death. He said people would much rather be the person in the casket than the person delivering the eulogy. But do you have to subscribe to that thinking?

A few months ago I was having breakfast with my brother and sister-in-law in Brisbane. She was telling me about their four-year-old daughter who had recently been in a dance concert performance on stage. She shared how her daughter came up to her and said, 'I'm so nervous about going on stage, Mum'. I imagine her mum had the same expression on her face as I did on hearing the story. This four-year-old has the charisma of Taylor Swift and the sass of Beyoncé, so there was no way she was nervous. Her mum looked at her and asked, 'Why? You like being on stage.' She replied, 'I don't know, but some of the other girls were saying it'. My sister-in-law said, 'You know it's okay to love being on stage, right?' Her daughter smiled, said 'Okay' and went happily on her way. It made me think about how we sometimes take on other people's beliefs even if they aren't that helpful to us.

As adults we do it all the time. Go and ask someone how they've been, and chances are they will say 'Busy'. Why? Because busy screams importance (even though none of us believe it). You might believe it takes seven years to digest gum or that you can't swim within an hour of eating, but it pays to check in and see if what you believe is actually helpful.

You've been thinking that public speaking is inherently stressful. You might hold the belief that you cannot stumble over your words or people will think you're no good. You might think that if people laugh at you then you've lost all credibility. But are these beliefs actually true or helping you?

REFRAME

Lead your thoughts.

The solution seems simple, right. *Don't think unhelpful thoughts.* Easy. Not really. I recently heard a friend of mine, Karen Williams, describe our brains as 'meaning making machines', with thoughts firing left, right and centre, thousands every day. Each thought is trying to make sense of the world around it, but unfortunately not every thought is going to be helpful, so don't believe everything you think.

Psychologists call these unhelpful thoughts *negative automatic thoughts*. When I was studying for my counselling degree we called them NATs, but I've since heard people call them

ANTs that need to be squashed (harsh but fair). What we know is that we cannot control our automatic thoughts; they are, by definition, *automatic*. But we don't have to believe everything we think. We can either be led by the brain and our automatic thoughts, or challenge them and lead the brain where we want to go and create more helpful thinking. We do this through the power of *reframing*.

In *Atomic Habits*, James Clear tells the story of a man he spoke to who was in a wheelchair. Asked how he handled being confined to a wheelchair, his response was that he wasn't *confined* to a wheelchair, he was *liberated* by it, because without it he wouldn't be able to go anywhere. What a beautiful illustration of the power of a *reframe*.

Let's look at this through two examples within the context of speaking.

Example 1

Someone introduces you to speak and the automatic thought pops into your head: *Don't stuff this up or everyone will think you're stupid.* You notice that thought and buy into it, and now you can't help but think about getting everything perfect and not making a mistake. As a result, even though you were once confident, you now feel the need to read directly from your notes and stumble your way through, because you didn't write out your presentation word for word.

Example 2

You are about to be introduced to speak and you look down and see your hands shaking. You immediately think, *I am so nervous! I hope I don't stuff this up.* Then, because you have told yourself how nervous you are, you start feeling sick, your neck gets stiff and your mouth goes dry.

These are two simple examples of being led by the brain. In his book *Cognitive Behaviour Therapy: Your Route Out of Perfectionism, Self-sabotage and Other Everyday Habits with CBT*, Avy Joseph explores three ways we can challenge dysfunctional thinking by asking questions:

1. **Evidence.** Is there a law or evidence to support this belief?

2. **Logic.** Does it make logical sense to think like this?

3. **Helpfulness.** How does believing this help you achieve what you want in the long term?

By asking these questions you will be able to challenge some of your negative automatic thoughts then reframe them using more helpful thinking. Let's look at these examples again.

Example 1

Someone introduces you to speak and the automatic thought pops into your head, *Don't stuff this up or everyone will think you're stupid.* You notice that thought and instead of buying into it you challenge and reframe it. You tell yourself, *Just because you make a mistake doesn't mean you're stupid.* You remind yourself that we are all imperfect, and you'll give it your best shot but it will be okay if it doesn't all go perfectly to plan. You take a deep breath and walk up confidently, just as you had prepared.

Example 2

You are about to be introduced to speak and you look down and see your hands shaking. You've done your research. You know your hands are shaking because of a rush of adrenalin through your body. It isn't because you are scared but because you are about to do something exciting. You use that energy to deliver with energy and enthusiasm.

Don't underestimate the value of a good reframe for unhelpful thinking.

REFOCUS

When you walk into the room, *focus on the right things*.

More often than not when we struggle with unhelpful thinking, we bring the focus back to ourselves or we direct it out to the people that intimidate us. We fall into the trap of comparison and ego.

Dealing with comparison

Comparison can be a confidence killer. It fills your mind with thoughts of someone else. I love this quote from Mike Robbins:

> *'What if we could expand our capacity for appreciating ourselves in a genuine way, and it has nothing to do with anything external? What if just being ourselves, the way we are right now, was good enough? Think of the freedom and peace we could experience in our lives (and have at times) by just being who we are – not trying to be what we think we're supposed to be, in order to get the things we think we're supposed to want.'*

One of our best weapons against unhelpful comparison is learning to be comfortable in our own skin. It takes a lot of work to appreciate who you are, and there's more to say on this than could ever fit into this book. If you are an analytical person, then own that. If you're funny, then be funny, but if you're not, don't feel pressured to be.

But let's be real. I have found that trying not to compare yourself with others is like trying not to think of a pink elephant. You're doing it right now, aren't you?

Everywhere we go, every day, we are surrounded by stimuli for comparison. We drive past a billboard and feel insecure about our body image. We open our social media and there's someone with a new job, house or car. We check LinkedIn and there's someone with a new program, promotion or opportunity that has us looking sideways rather than running our own race.

It seems almost impossible to escape comparison. But what if, rather than trying to escape it, we decided to use it to produce something good in us? What if there was a better side of comparison? What would it look like? Perhaps, rather than bitter regret, it would look like a determination to get better. Rather than comparing yourself with another person's talents and getting discouraged, what if you chose to look at the good qualities you aspire to and decided to work on improving yourself?

Comparison moves into dangerous territory when it produces in us the desire for something we cannot attain or should not aspire to. If comparison has a better side, it should bring out the best in us, not the worst. It should help us become the best version of ourselves rather than a carbon copy of someone else. It should never make us feel inferior. It should inspire us to be the best we can be.

Getting above the line

What if I stumble over my words or make a mistake?

What if I lose the respect of my peers or leaders?

What if I haven't prepared enough?

What if I go blank or forget what I have to say?

Whether you have been asked to present to the senior leadership team, to speak to your team or to deliver a speech at a wedding, you will find that many of your internal conversations have one common denominator.

They focus on you.

Sometimes it isn't a *confidence* problem we have; it's a *focus* problem.

When explaining it to the people I work with I often compare it to walking into a room with your phone's 'selfie' camera turned on. We are often front and centre in the picture. *Note:* I once said this in a training room and the biggest revelation to those in the room was that their phone had a front-facing camera. But most of the time the illustration works.

It's okay. We all do it. I catch myself slipping into these moments too. There's usually a couple of signs that alert me that there's an issue with my focus and it's becoming about me. When it becomes about me, I'll drift down below the line; when I make it about others I rise above the line. Figure 11 shows what it looks like when we operate above or below the line.

Figure 11: Communicating in service

SERVICE	How can I help?
SUPPORT	How can this help?

- -

STRUCTURE	How does this look?
STATUS	How do I look?

Status

When the focus is on me, I'm preoccupied with my *status*. I ask, 'How do I look?' It's not just about my physical appearance, but about how I might be perceived by the people in the room.

In these moments I'm tempted to let *pride* sneak in. The danger is that I'm less likely to expose my vulnerabilities and more likely to focus on my accomplishments to win people over. People might be inspired by my victories, but they connect through my battles.

Structure

When the focus is on me, I'm obsessed with my *structure*. I ask, 'How does this look?' Have I prepared enough? How will I open? What will I say?

In these moments I can fall into the trap of *perfectionism*. Going through what I will say, line by line, with more focus on the notes in front of me than the people around me. Maybe even stepping away from the room in those crucial moments before I have to get up, to go over my outline one more time.

When I see any of these signs, I know it's time to shift my focus. This means an intentional decision to refocus.

Here is what I have discovered happens when I intentionally refocus and make it about others.

Support

When the focus is on others, I'm not just asking how this looks, I'm asking, 'How does this help?' How does what I'm sharing support these people to do their job better? How does this build up the people I am speaking to? How can this message benefit the people I am speaking to?

In these moments I'm more focused on being *helpful*. How can I learn from the people in the room, adapt my content to support the decisions they have to make and solve the problems they face?

Service

When the focus is on others, I'm not just asking how do I look, I'm asking, 'How can I help?'

I focus on the people I have the privilege of speaking to and ask, 'How can I be of service?' How can I bring the best of me to bring out the best of you? And what do you need most from me?

In these moments I'm focused on being *humble*. It's been said that humility isn't thinking less of yourself but thinking of yourself less. When you walk into the room, make a personal commitment to serve the people in the room.

I've said it already, but I'll say it again. If as a leader you can gain control over your thoughts, you'll gain control over your life. Recognise your unhelpful thoughts, reframe them and refocus on the important things. Better thinking is critical to better leading.

CHAPTER 10
GET BETTER AT INVESTING

If you want to see a return, you need to make an *investment*. Leadership investment is active, not passive.

When I was a child, I used to sneak into my brother's bedroom when he was out. Like most siblings, he was extremely territorial about his room, but I couldn't help but succumb to temptation every time he would leave the house, because I knew that waiting on the other side of his door was his acoustic guitar. I had failed most instruments I tried to learn, to the point where my music teacher refused to teach me anything more because I lacked commitment to an instrument. Perhaps it was the danger of getting caught that made playing my brother's guitar so exciting, but I couldn't wait for him to leave the house so I could sneak in. I would hold the guitar in my hand and play the first few notes of 'Nothing Else Matters' by Metallica. I use 'play' loosely, because it only required me to pluck a few of the bottom strings without actually needing to know any chords. After a few busts and beatings from my brother, I was finally gifted my own guitar and started to teach myself how to play. It didn't take too long to realise that it was *really* hard. My fingertips were raw and aching, and sheet music was another language to me. Yet over the next few years I practised and invested and, not so surprisingly, got a lot better. I wouldn't call myself a prodigy by any stretch of the imagination, but I can fairly claim I now know how to play the guitar.

If you want to build confidence and develop your leadership and communication, then you need to get better at investing in and sharpening your skills. Here are a few ways to do this that I have found valuable.

INVEST IN YOUR CONNECTIONS

Be intentional about the people you surround yourself with.

It's fascinating how much you pick up from the people around you, but be mindful that this includes both the good and the bad.

Two people I know who grew up together worked for the same leader. They regularly listened to that leader speak, and he always opened the same way. When I heard my friends speak at two different events it was like watching copies of that leader. They both started in exactly the same way, and the resemblance in some of their mannerisms was uncanny.

Leaders who grow are intentional about the people they spend their time with. Jim Rohn has famously suggested that you are 'the average of the five people you spend the most time with'. If you want to get better, spend time with people who are better than you. Or, as the popular saying goes, 'If you're the smartest person in the room, find a new room'.

Leaders grow in *community*. If you want to grow, whether in communication or leadership, surround yourself with a community that will enlarge both your network and your thinking.

Leaders grow from *wisdom and experience*. Find someone further along on the journey and invest time in them. Don't underestimate the value of finding the right mentor or coach.

Leaders grow through *observation*. Not all mentoring requires a personal relationship. Some can help you grow through a screen, curriculum or book. Ask yourself some simple questions:

- Who am I growing with? (community)
- Who am I learning from? (experience)
- Who am I gleaning from? (observation)

INVEST YOUR TIME WISELY

Invest your time as you would invest your money, and watch how differently you'll spend it.

Leaders who grow are committed to doing the work needed to get better, and this is reflected in their priorities. What are you saying *yes* to that will help you become more of who you want to be? What are you saying *no* to that is taking you away from where you want to be?

Leaders grow when they invest time in gaining knowledge and skills. It's important to take time to read books, articles and research to expand your thinking. Listen to podcasts and watch videos of people who provoke and inspire you to think beyond your normal boundaries.

INVEST IN PREPARATION AND PRACTICE

Leaders grow when they invest in preparation and practice, because *practice makes progress*. Practice is what separates an average musician, athlete or leader from an expert. Take time to hone, refine and develop your skills or craft. Say yes to speaking or taking on new opportunities that allow you to get your hands dirty and have a go.

Next time someone asks for a volunteer to say a few words at an event, why not put your hand up? When someone needs to present the figures to the board, take the lead and have a go.

You will grow when you invest time in building your capability. Go out and find training opportunities or courses that will build your capability and close the skills gap. Be willing to invest in your future, because it's worth it.

Practice and preparation are fundamental for building your confidence as a communicator. One of the common questions I am asked is, 'How much should I practise?' It's been said that Steve Jobs rehearsed and agonised for days and even weeks in the lead-up to his most notable presentations. Dr Jill Bolte Taylor has told Carmine Gallo, author of *Talk Like TED*, that she rehearsed more than 200 times before standing up to deliver her popular TED talk 'My Stroke of Insight'. It takes quite a lot of effort to make something look effortless. A ballerina flies gracefully through the air, a diver plunges 25 metres to enter the water without making a splash, yet what they make look easy is the product of countless hours of preparation and practice.

The amount of practice will differ from person to person, but the quality of delivery is *always* linked to the depth of preparation. So how long should you practise? Personally, I practise for as long as it takes me to dig through three key layers (see Figure 12).

Figure 12: Three layers of preparation

CLARITY	*Flow*
CONNECTION	*Feel*
CONVICTION	*Fire*

Layer #1: Finding clarity

At the foundational level, my practice is about finding clarity. I want to know what I'm going to say and how I will say it. When practising, I take all the time I need to go through my presentation until I am able to move seamlessly through the key elements. I think through my process and find my transitional statements. Like changing gears in a car, it usually starts a bit clunkily, but eventually I'll find my rhythm and flow. I practise out loud, not just in my head, until I can deliver the presentation without relying on my notes or slides.

The question I ask myself here is, *Does this flow?*

Layer #2: Finding connection

As I take my preparation deeper, I start looking beyond flow for something to connect with. I want to *feel* something. I want to understand why this matters to me. I think about the people who will be listening and why it matters to them. I'm looking for the key elements that I connect with, that inspire me and make me feel passionate about the idea. I'm not just looking to deliver something that has structure. I want it to have emotion.

The question I'm asking myself here is, *How does this feel?*

Layer #3: Finding conviction

There's a shift that takes place when I commit to putting in the effort and taking the time to dig deep. It's a shift from *I know this* to *I believe this*. It's the powerful combination of head and heart. At the start I'm speaking because I have to, but by the time I finish I'm speaking because I need to. I can't stay silent for a moment longer because this idea has lit a fire inside me.

This level of practice is about taking the time to build conviction in what you have to share. The question I'm asking myself here is, *Have I found the fire?*

As I prepare:

- I practise until I get the *clarity* – I want it to *flow*.

- I practise until I get the *connection* – I want to *feel* it.

- But deep down I practise until I get the *conviction* – I want it to burn like a *fire* inside me because I believe in it so deeply.

So how long should you practise? What's the magic number? I think that all depends on how deep you want to go.

As a business leader you might be wondering if a presentation on your reward and recognition program really needs *conviction*. Perhaps it doesn't. You may not always have the time to dig deep in this kind of way. I would say, however, that people will struggle to believe your message if you don't do a minimum amount of work to get to that place.

Equally, there will be times when too much preparation can itself become a trap.

THE PREPARATION TRAP

Holding the door for someone is courteous, but holding a revolving door for someone won't be so well received. Revolving doors are designed to allow entry and exit when walked through. You definitely don't want to be trapped in them. Think about preparation in the same way. It's about moving your key message and idea *through* the process of preparation towards the goal of delivery – from ideation to execution. If we aren't careful it can be all too easy to find ourselves caught up in the process.

Take these three examples (see Figure 13).

Figure 13: The revolving door of preparation

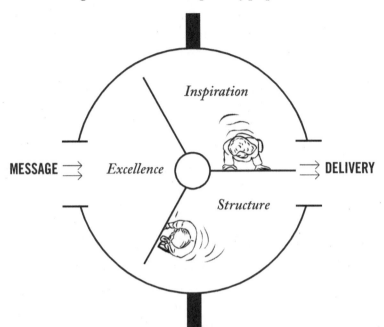

Excellence

Leaders choose excellence over mediocrity. What leader wants to deliver something average? But this dedication to excellence can trigger an insatiable need for *perfection*. The unrealistic goal of the 'perfect' presentation can lead to a never-ending spin around the revolving door.

To avoid the perfection trap, at each stage of preparation ask yourself, *Have I given my best to this?* If the answer is yes, move on through.

Inspiration

Seeking out inspiration from other speakers, experts or authors is a great way to build perspective and awareness on a topic. But the quickest way to kill something special is to compare it with something else. *Comparison* can be a never-ending trip in a revolving door because it is never fully satisfied. People want to connect with you, but they can't do that when you spend all your time trying to be someone else.

To avoid the comparison trap, *ask why did they* more than *how did they*. Take the time to examine the motivation and not just the application. Learn from everyone, but don't copy anyone.

Structure

Structure is a great roadmap, but what happens when things don't go to plan? What will you do if a 25-minute presentation is cut short to just five? Planning and creating structure is a necessary process to move through, but relying too much on structure can create *inflexibility*. Create a structure rigid enough to chart the course, but ensure you stay flexible enough to adjust it as you go.

To avoid the inflexibility trap, tell yourself, *If I achieve nothing else, I must* _____. Determine what message *must* be communicated in the event that you aren't able to share all you *want* to communicate.

Preparation is an important and necessary process to move *through* but it is not something to get stuck *in*. Be careful not to allow helpful activities to transition into unhelpful cycles.

Developing means investing. Surround yourself with high-calibre people, be intentional with your time, practise and dig deep in your preparation (but don't get stuck there).

When I had just turned 20, I was told that the best investment I could make was in property. 'You can't fail when you invest in property,' they told me. Sometime later I was told the best investment I could make was in shares. 'You can never lose when you invest in shares,' they insisted. Years later I was told the best investment I could make was in cryptocurrency. 'If you get in now you can't lose,' they told me. I now get emails promising me I'll receive a long-lost inheritance once I send them my bank details.

While we may share different investment game plans and opinions, there's one strategy we should all agree is the *best investment*. It's not houses, or shares, crypto or your email inheritance. It's, quite simply, *you*.

I have always found the best return on investment is one that moves you closer to the best version of you. And the best version of you is the greatest gift you can give to your family, your friends and your team.

CHAPTER 11
GET BETTER AT ASKING

Good leaders don't have all the answers, but they know how to ask the right questions. I've found that leaders who are committed to growth aren't afraid to ask the challenging questions. They are intentional in the conversations they have both with themselves and with others.

Leaders grow from purposeful consideration. Have you taken time to consider the type of leader you want to be and the kinds of things you value most?

Leaders grow from personal reflection. What type of leader are you now? How does this align with the type of leader you *want* to be?

Leaders grow from helpful feedback. What type of leader do others say you are? What are your blind spots? Who do you trust to tell you what you need to hear, not just what you want to hear?

You can't grow from the things you don't know.

Early on in my journey speaking to large groups of people I had an annoying habit. To be honest, I probably had many, but this particular one frustrated a lot of people who listened to me speak. The problem was I was completely unaware of it.

Have you ever arrived home after a day of meetings to discover a giant piece of food (it's almost always green) lodged between your front teeth and thought to yourself, *why didn't anyone tell me!* Every time I got to speak, I had the metaphorical equivalent to that piece of food between my front teeth that everyone could see except me. One day a good friend approached me with some feedback. In this glass-shattering moment, he pointed out the habit and it instantly became visible to me. I couldn't believe I hadn't notice it sooner. As painful as the revelation was, I realised immediately how significant it was in helping me become a better communicator. It reinforced for me the insight that 'you can't grow from the things you don't know'.

There's no argument that feedback is critical to leadership growth because it holds up a mirror to our blind spots and shows us where we need to get better. However, there are decisions we can make to leverage feedback and accelerate our leadership growth. I have found that the fastest pathway for growth and progress is when feedback is both *intentionally sought* and *openly embraced*.

INTENTIONALLY SOUGHT FEEDBACK

When it comes to feedback, there are those who wait for it and those who *seek* it. Those who experience the fastest growth intentionally seek out feedback. Time spent waiting for feedback to find us is time spent unconsciously reinforcing bad habits or behaviour. Those who actively and consistently seek feedback nip bad behaviour in the bud before it begins to take root. It's the equivalent of asking someone, 'Is there anything stuck in my teeth?' before spending a day in meetings puzzling over a lot of awkward stares.

Valuable feedback is best sought from people you trust. Having spent time as a graphic designer, I know as well as most that everyone has an opinion and some are not shy in sharing theirs. If you take on everyone's feedback you can find yourself thrown all over the place. The key is to seek feedback from a trusted source who has demonstrated credibility. Find a mentor or someone who models the characteristics you would like to develop and ask them a few simple questions such as:

- What can you see that I could do differently to make more progress right now?

- What can you see me doing that I might not be able to see right now?

- What would you like to say to me that you think I need to hear?

Ask the audience

When you want to have a go and you don't have access to a coach or trusted adviser, who do you ask? How do you learn when there isn't someone there focused on observing you? How can you elicit feedback on your presentation or meeting that goes beyond the typical 'it was great, thanks', while avoiding the unhelpful and misinformed feedback of the overzealous?

The answer is actually simple. Who better to ask than your audience? Asking the right questions of your audience can give huge insight into areas of personal improvement.

It's also possible to get the feedback in a positive and inconspicuous way. Here are three questions you can ask someone in your audience after your presentation to identify personal growth areas.

Question #1: In your words, what was the key message?

This is a question of *clarity*.

Every effective meeting or presentation should communicate a clear message. Speaking is not just saying something but having something valuable to say. No matter how many subpoints or ideas are included, they should all point towards the *one big idea* you are trying to communicate.

If you ask an audience or team member to summarise your presentation and the key message they identify is different from the one you intended to convey, then there is an issue of clarity that you need to address next time.

Question #2: What parts did you find most engaging?

This is a question of *delivery*.

What memorable moments can your audience recall? What did and did not work will quickly become apparent from what people found most engaging and what they struggled to recall. The topics or approaches we think are most valuable are not always those that are most engaging for the audience. This can help guide how much time we allocate to certain topics in future delivery.

Question #3: What will you do differently?

This is a question of *practicality*.

What's the take home? What is your next step from here? As people leave your meeting or presentation, what will they do differently? To leave people inspired is great; to leave people changed is far better. When preparing to speak, a leader should think, *What do I want people to do after hearing this?* If audience members' answers differ from your intended outcomes, then you've just found a great opportunity to learn and grow.

Don't just ask someone, 'How did I do?' Ask intentional questions that leave no room for subjective interpretation. Hold the opinion of the crowd loosely, but have the posture of a student in every way you can.

OPENLY EMBRACED FEEDBACK

While it's important to seek out feedback, we also need to be open to receiving what is being said. We all understand it is valuable, but feedback isn't always easy to hear. Growth requires change, and where there is change there is pain. The harder we have to work to change a behaviour or habit, the more painful that process becomes. It also requires a high degree of humility to recognise that there are some things we just don't know, especially when others seem to know more than we do. Leaders understand that in order to continue growing we need to be humble enough to acknowledge our blind spots. If we are intentional about asking for feedback but refuse to listen when it is given, we self-sabotage our own growth.

Here are three feedback mindsets I try to adopt whenever I am receiving feedback that may be painful.

1. **I need this to grow.** I want to grow and can't grow from the things I don't know. This will make me bigger and better.

2. **This is not an attack.** It's about what I'm doing, not who I am. I value what is said and don't need to be defensive. Even if I disagree, there is something here I can learn.

3. **This person values me enough to say something.** Giving feedback is sometimes as difficult as receiving it. If someone gives me feedback, it shows me they care about my development.

You can't grow from the things you don't know. The pathway to fast growth is being intentional about discovering these things, openly embracing feedback and making positive change. A coach or mentor is a great way to fast-track this growth.

If you want to develop, you need to get better at first asking the right questions and then, even more important, applying the feedback you receive.

CHAPTER 12
GET BETTER AT FAILING

Every leader needs to know how to get better at failing.

When a professional athlete commits to excelling at their sport, they know they are going to have some setbacks along the way. Perhaps it's the loss of an important match or an injury sustained while playing. They also know they will never achieve the joy of a win if they succumb to the pain of a defeat. They know, in other words, how to fail forward.

It's unrealistic to think that in leadership too you won't experience some pain or failure along the way. Just as the athlete must learn how to play through the pain, you will need to know how to lead beyond failure.

Have you noticed how some people experience this kind of failure and continue to thrive and progress, while others who face the same setbacks struggle to recover? It's because the former group have learned how to *fail better*.

Failure is an inevitable part of any leader's journey. So the question becomes not *if* you will fail, but *how*. Here are seven insights I have gained about people who seem to fail better, and seven questions I have learned to ask when navigating through these waters myself.

1. They accept it

They accept that failure is a normal part of the process.

It doesn't surprise them when they fail. They understand that not everything you do will work out the way you expect, and they are content with that. They aren't afraid to take risks and try something that hasn't been done. They accept that sometimes you win and other times you learn.

Question #1: Is the fear of failure stopping me from trying?

2. They recognise it

They recognise when something isn't working.

This can be hard to see. When you are passionate about an idea, you want it to work and you don't want to give up on it too soon. As a result, it's easy to spend more time and resources keeping something on life support that we should have let go a long time ago. People who fail better know how to recognise when something needs to change before it is too late.

Question #2: What isn't working right now that I need to stop?

3. They own it

They take responsibility for their part and take ownership of what needs to change.

People who fail better aren't looking for someone to blame when something goes wrong, even when it would be easy to do so. Even if the failure was beyond their control, they take responsibility for their contribution. They know you cannot change what you are unwilling to own. Ownership of a failure does not mean you personally are a failure. It is about taking ownership of your actions, not taking ownership of an identity.

Question #3: What part did I play in this not working?

4. They learn from it

They find every opportunity to learn and grow.

People who fail better treat failure as a teacher. They know there is a lesson to be learned and work hard to find it. When they learn, they apply the knowledge and grow. When something doesn't work, they want to know why – not so they can point a finger or pass the blame, but so they can avoid making the same mistake again. To make a mistake is okay; to repeat the same mistake is not.

Question #4: What can I learn and how can I grow from this?

5. They share it

They share their learning and experience with others.

It seems strange that you would want to promote your failure. But those who fail better don't see it as promoting failure; they see it as helping others avoid the same mistakes. They know that if they can help others avoid the same mistakes, they are contributing to the broader success of the organisation. By sharing their failures, they know they are helping others move forward faster.

Question #5: How can this experience help others?

6. They change it

They make the necessary adjustments to position themselves for success.

When something isn't working, it needs to change. People who fail better learn from their experiences and make the necessary adjustments to better position themselves for future success. Sometimes these adjustments are obvious, and other times they need some input from those outside the process. They aren't intimidated by asking for help; they know that the best bet for success is tapping into the best of those around them.

Question #6: What can I do differently this time?

7. They move forward from it

They keep moving forward.

While others sit around wallowing in their failure, these leaders know how to keep moving forward. Failure is a part of the process, not the end of it. They understand that failure does not need to be final. They let go of the pain or frustration of the past event and, armed with the lessons and experience they have gained, step forward into the future opportunity.

Question #7: What is stopping me from moving forward?

These are some of the insights I have gained from observing leaders who seem to fail better. This isn't about the pursuit of failure in order to achieve success. Rather, it's about recognising that the pursuit of growth will inevitably include moments of failure. It's how you respond to these challenges that makes the difference.

Failing is okay. Be the type of leader who fails better.

WHERE TO NOW?

The idea of being *there* is extremely alluring. The end game, the end of a process, the successful accomplishment of a goal. The problem is that most of the time I'm not there, I'm here. And usually when I finally get there I find myself in another here and looking towards a brand-new there!

Imagine starting out with all the skills and expertise of a professional athlete without having to do all the training and exercise. Imagine thinking about writing a book then, *BAM!*, the book is written and edited and designed and published and sitting right in front of you without all the gruelling days and nights of writing and all the production work. What if you went to bed one night and woke up the next morning and looked in the mirror and there was that six-pack you've been craving without all that stupid diet and exercise? Sounds like a dream, doesn't it? We know deep down that it is unrealistic to expect ourselves to arrive *there* if we haven't put in the work.

Do you ever find yourself comparing your here to someone else's there? I sure have. I've sat in conferences and heard speakers who make me want to quit speaking. I've read books from leaders that made me panic-stricken at the thought of publishing my own book, knowing it would never be as good as theirs. Have you ever found yourself just a little discouraged about your here when you look at someone else's there?

What I have learned over time is that all those people I admire (and even at times compare myself against) didn't start out *there*. Long before J.K. Rowling became one of the world's biggest-selling authors she laboured away in obscurity, working late nights, skipping meals so her daughter could eat in times of 'literally no money'. Long before the rise of his multibillion-dollar conglomerate or pioneering work in commercial space travel, Richard Branson was selling records out of the boot of his car. Long before Steve Jobs took to the stage to launch technology that would literally transform the global digital landscape, he was working out of a garage in Los Altos, California.

You don't start *there*, you start *here*.

When I delivered one of my first presentations, my shaking hands clutched an A4 page of notes covering all kinds of unrelated topics. I didn't know how to string together a simple argument, so I went with the mantra of quantity over quality. Today I have very little difficulty in standing up in front of a room without any notes and at times with very little notice. I didn't start there. I worked my way up. Now I look at others... and realise I still have a long way to go.

Where to now? My answer is simple: start here and then take your first step towards there. Do you want to develop your character, to build your credibility, to gain more clarity in your messaging? Take what you have and do the work needed to take your next step.

Growth is not so much one giant leap as a series of small next steps. Getting to the place you want to be isn't going to happen overnight; it's going to take time and investment. You don't have to do everything – just start with something.

Maybe this means:

- saying *yes* instead of *no* the next time you're asked to speak

- phoning up a coach and asking for some help

- sitting down and figuring out on paper what you want to be known for

- rethinking how you could make the next message you deliver more succinct and stimulating.

Whatever it is for you, just start where you are. Start before you think you're ready, when you don't feel like you've figured it all out yet, when you still lack confidence, when you don't feel like you measure up. Just start.

In writing this book, I've aimed higher than just helping people become better speakers. My objective is to help build more effective leaders. Because in the moments that matter people aren't just looking *for something* that can inform them, they are looking *to someone* who will lead them. I really hope that next time you stand up on your platform, whatever that may look like, you'll see it as more than an opportunity to speak to the room; rather, you'll see it as an opportunity to *Lead the Room*. Every moment matters. Use it as an opportunity to say something that truly counts.

A FLIGHT PATH EXAMPLE

In a public program I ran I was workshopping a presentation with the group. The topic they chose was 'reward and recognition'. One of the participants had recently received the results of his employee engagement survey and wanted to use this as an opportunity to talk to the team about creating a culture of reward and recognition. I thought this would be an appropriate topic to demonstrate how I would approach a presentation on reward and recognition and our work together in the program.

THE VALUE

'Reward and recognition' is a big, broad topic. We first need to get clear on why we are delivering this to our team and what the value is. There will be problems relating to employee engagement and problems around people's solutions. We needed to explore the problems the audience might experience and determine value by addressing these problems.

1. Boardroom problems
Employee engagement
- Low scores on staff survey
- Low morale
- Poor culture
- Stress-related injury and high turnover

Reward and recognition

- Lack of time to recognise everything people do
- No budget or resources to make it happen

2. Bedroom problems

Employee engagement

- Do people like working here? For me?
- Are team members with us?
- Why bother showing up if nobody appreciates me?
- Do people even care?

Reward and recognition

- I never get recognised for the work I do.
- Am I doing a good job?
- I don't know where to start.
- I barely have time to get my own job done.

THE MESSAGE

What is the one thing you want people to know when they leave, and how can you communicate it succinctly? When we workshopped the message, the group reached a consensus on wanting people to know that reward and recognition were not complex or time consuming. This was one of the big discoveries when discussing the value. We wanted people to know that a little recognition could go a long way in helping to lift the employee experience. We understood that initial reservations people had towards reward and recognition revolved mainly around time and cost. Collectively we agreed on the key message:

> 'Reward and recognition doesn't take long, but it does go a long way.'

This message highlighted the idea that with just a small investment of time, the team could see real change take place.

THE PLAN

Once we were clear on our message, we started to build the plan to deliver it with the most impact.

1. Attention

What will make people pay attention to what we have to say?

Ask an intentional question

- When have you felt most valued at work?
- How do you know if you're doing a good job?
- What percentage of people do you think are engaged at work in your organisation? (You could share the results of the staff survey.)

Make an audacious statement

- If we all do one thing better, we can transform our organisation.

Share a purposeful story

- Share a professional story about how recognition for a job you completed made you feel at work.

Throw an unexpected curve ball

- Show a video story of someone on the team then take a moment to recognise and reward their work in front of the team.

2. Tension

How can you give people a reason to stay engaged? Take a moment to consider some of the problems we discussed earlier and how they can create tension for people.

Highlight the problem

- Share a story about a time when you felt undervalued for the work you had done so as to relate with people in the room.

- Ask people if they have ever felt doubts about whether they are doing a good job.

Highlight the question

- Create a knowledge gap by asking people to consider what activity they think could lift employee engagement.

- Address some finance-related problems by telling people you are going to show them how to increase engagement while also reducing costs to the business.

Highlight the vision

- Describe in detail what your workplace would look like with an effective culture of reward and recognition. What would look different if you showed up to work tomorrow and people were doing what you wanted them to do?

3. Perspective

We now want to help people get a clearer perspective of what we are talking about by looking at the big idea through four different lenses.

Make a list of your key texts

- Gallup's *State of the Global Workplace* survey, which found that just 13 per cent of employees are engaged at work.
- *HBR* article on study finding that 40 per cent of employees say they would work harder if their employer recognised them more often.

Consider how you can translate these

- Ten people in a boat and only one person is rowing.
- You finish a marathon because you know there's a reward at the end.

Write down some of your key thoughts

- People who don't know if they are doing a good job are less likely to be engaged at work.
- We have a responsibility to help people know when they kick a goal and to reward them when they finish a race.

Consider what you would like people to take away

- Include two cost-effective ways managers can reward and recognise someone on their team right now.
- Give people a handout with some ideas and tactics around reward and recognition.

4. Resolution

Consider the question 'What then?'

Drive home your key message:

> *'Recognition doesn't take long, but it does go a long way.'*

Frame it

- 'The one thing I want you to remember is…'

- 'What is most important to remember is…'
- 'The big idea here is that…'

5. Action

Consider the question 'What if?'

What would happen if everyone did what you were asking of them?

- Reinforce the compelling vision you introduced earlier.
- Describe in detail what it would look like if the problems were solved.

Consider the question 'What next?'

What do you want people to do right now? It could be as simple as:

- Take a moment to write down a note of thanks to someone who has done something great, then share it with the person as you leave.
- Keep a lookout for an email with a reward and recognition fact sheet we are going to send to you later today.

ABOUT THE AUTHOR

Shane Hatton has spent his career in the business of people. From his early days in event management, recruiting and mobilising large volunteer teams for community events, he has navigated the challenges of leading at scale. Knowing how difficult it can be to get one on one with everyone, he has learned the value of leveraging a communication platform to build trust and rally people around a common vision. From more than a decade of consulting and in-house experience in marketing and communications he has learned the importance of effective messaging to not only be heard but remembered.

Shane also spent seven years as a minister. During this time, he was leading and mobilising volunteers in one of Australia's fastest growing churches and responsible for building and nurturing the health, growth and culture of a rapidly expanding campus. This experience at the intersection of people, communication and leadership, along with his studies in business and psychology, laid the foundation for his work today as a trainer, mentor and speaker to leaders and teams.

Shane knows the deep satisfaction of standing in front of a team of people, watching the lights go on, knowing they are with you; at the same time, he understands the sense of panic that can take hold when all eyes are on you in those crucial moments. A self-described 'charismatic introvert', he has learned how to face the fear of public speaking and embrace the potential of platform leadership.

He has always believed that great communication is much bigger than 'speaking', that it must be viewed through the lens of leadership – and it is this perspective he brings to bear in *Lead the Room*.

If you're looking for Shane in his down time, you'll likely find him buried in a good book or surrounded by good friends where great coffee can be found.

If you'd like to read more of Shane's work on how to step up, take charge and Lead the Room, subscribe at shanemhatton.com.

SOURCES

Arcadi, J. (2015). *Clearing the Mist In the Pulpit: On Analytic Theology for Preaching.* [online]. Available at: http://analytictheology.fuller.edu/clearing-the-mist-in-the-pulpit-on-analytic-theology-for-preaching/

Baldoni, J. (2008). *Leader's Credibility Is Golden.* [online] hbr.org. Available at: https://hbr.org/2008/11/leaders-credibility-is-golden

Bersin, J. (2016). *Good Presentations Need to Make People Uncomfortable.* [online] hbr.org. Available at: https://hbr.org/2016/09/good-presentations-need-to-make-people-uncomfortable

Brouk, T. (2018). *To Give a Great Presentation, Distill Your Message to Just 15 Words.* [online] hbr.org. Available at: https://hbr.org/2018/11/to-give-a-great-presentation-distill-your-message-to-just-15-words

Church, M. (2013). *Amplifiers: Using the Power of Motivational Leadership to Inspire and Influence Others.* Wiley.

Clear, J. (2018). *Atomic Habits: Tiny Changes, Remarkable Results: An Easy & Proven Way to Build Good Habits & Break Bad Ones.* Random House Business Books.

CliftonStrengths®. https://www.gallupstrengthscenter.com/home/en-us/cliftonstrengths-themes-domains

Cohan, J. & Luna, T. (2017). *To Get People to Change, Make Change Easy.* [online] hbr.org. Available at: https://hbr.org/2017/12/to-get-people-to-change-make-change-easy

Curran, T. & Hill, A. (2018). *Perfectionism Is Increasing, and That's Not Good News.* [online] hbr.org. Available at: https://hbr.org/2018/01/perfectionism-is-increasing-and-thats-not-good-news

Duarte, N. (2012). *Five Presentation Mistakes Everyone Makes.* [online] hbr.org. Available at: https://hbr.org/2012/12/avoid-these-five-mistakes-in-y

The Economic Times, India. https://economictimes.indiatimes.com/small-biz/startups/a-timeline-of-uber-ceo-travis-kalanicks-bumpy-ride/articleshow/59253712.cms

Edelman Trust Barometer: Global Report (2018). Available at: https://www.edelman.com/sites/g/files/aatuss191/files/2018-10/2018_Edelman_Trust_Barometer_Global_Report_FEB.pdf

Fuscaldo, D. (2013). *Why Employees Love Their CEO's.* [online] Glass Door. Available at: https://www.glassdoor.com/employers/blog/what-makes-employees-love-their-ceo

Gallo, C. (2016). *How Storytelling Hooks Your Audience.* [online] Available at: https://www.forbes.com/sites/carminegallo/2016/02/16/how-storytelling-hooks-your-audience/#41f84624413b

Gallo, C. (2014). *9 Public-Speaking Lessons from the World's Greatest TED Talks.* [online] Available at: https://www.forbes.com/sites/carminegallo/2014/03/04/9-public-speaking-lessons-from-the-worlds-greatest-ted-talks/#7537b0414a9d

Godin, S. (2002). *Purple Cow: Transform Your Business by Being Remarkable.* Portfolio.

Heath, C. & Heath, D. (2006). *Made to Stick: Why Some Ideas Survive and Others Die.* Random House.

Hoffeld, D. (2016). *The Science of Selling: Proven Strategies to Make Your Pitch, Influence Decisions, and Close the Deal.* TarcherPerigee.

IP Australia. https://www.ipaustralia.gov.au/trade-marks/ understanding-trade-marks/types-of-trade-marks

Joseph, A. (2009). *Cognitive Behaviour Therapy: Your Route out of Perfectionism, Self-Sabotage and Other Everyday Habits with CBT.* Capstone, Wiley.

Kyodo (2018). *Reira Iwabuchi crashes during final run, finishes fourth in Big Air.* [online] *Japan Times.* Available at: https://www.japantimes.co.jp/sports/2018/02/22/ olympics/winter-olympics/olympics-snowboarding/ reira-iwabuchi-crashes-final-run-finishes-fourth-big-air

Loewenstein, G. (1994). 'The Psychology of Curiosity: A Review and Reinterpretation'. *Psychological Bulletin*, 116, 75–98.

Macintyre, P. D. & Thivierge, K. (1995). 'The Effects of Speaker Personality on Anticipated Reactions to Public Speaking'. *Communication Research Reports*, 12, 125–33.

Maister, D., Green, H. & Galford, R. (2000). *The Trusted Advisor.* New York: Free Press.

Maxwell, J. C. (2005). *Developing the Leaders Around You.* Nashville, TN: Nelson Business.

McCord, P. (2017). *Powerful: Building a Culture of Freedom and Responsibility: From the Co-creator of NETFLIX Culture Deck.* Silicon Guild.

McSpadden, K. (2015). 'You Now Have a Shorter Attention Span Than a Goldfish'. [online] time.com. Available at: http://time.com/3858309/attention-spans-goldfish/

NBN Co, https://www.nbnco.com.au/blog/connected- homes/on-track-for-over-30-iot-devices-per-aussie- household-by-2021

Newton, Elizabeth. (1990). *The Rocky Road from Actions to Intentions*. Stanford University.

Nicas, J. (2018). *Apple Is Worth $1,000,000,000,000. Two Decades Ago, It Was Almost Bankrupt*. [online]. *The New York Times*. Available at: https://www.nytimes.com/2018/08/02/technology/apple-stock-1-trillion-market-cap.html

Novet, J. (2018). *How Satya Nadella tripled Microsoft's stock price in just over four years*. [online] cnbc.com. Available at: https://www.cnbc.com/2018/07/17/how-microsoft-has-evolved-under-satya-nadella.html

Parekh, R. (2012). *After 50 Years, Avis Drops Iconic 'We Try Harder' Tagline*. [online]. AdAge. Available at: https://adage.com/article/news/50-years-avis-drops-iconic-harder-tagline/236887

Porter, J. (2017). *Why You Should Make Time for Self-Reflection (Even If You Hate Doing It)*. [online] hbr.org. Available at: https://hbr.org/2017/03/why-you-should-make-time-for-self-reflection-even-if-you-hate-doing-it

Rath, T. (2015). *Are You Fully Charged?: The 3 Keys to Energizing Your Work and Life*. Silicon Guild, an Imprint of Missionday.

Rister, A. (2012). *The Ingredients of an Effective Slide*. [online]. Available at: https://alexrister1.wordpress.com/2012/06/14/

Robbins, M. (2009). *Just Be You*. [online] Mike Robbins. Available at: https://mike-robbins.com/just-be-you

Ronson, J. (2015). *How One Stupid Tweet Blew Up Justine Sacco's Life*. [online] *The New York Times*. Available at: www.nytimes.com/2015/02/15/magazine/how-one-stupid-tweet-ruined-justine-saccos-life.html

Seppälä, E. & King, M. (2017). *Burnout at Work Isn't Just About Exhaustion. It's Also About Loneliness*. [online] hbr.org. Available at: https://hbr.org/2017/06/burnout-at-work-isnt-just-about-exhaustion-its-also-about-loneliness

Simon, A. (1971), 'Designing Organizations for an Information-Rich World', in Martin Greenberger (ed.), *Computers, Communications, and the Public Interest,* Johns Hopkins, pp. 37–72.

Simons, D. & Chabris, C. (1999). 'Gorillas in our midst: Sustained inattentional blindness for dynamic events', *Perception,* 28, 1059–74.

Simons, T. (2002). *The High Cost of Lost Trust.* [online] hbr.org. Available at: https://hbr.org/2002/09/the-high-cost-of-lost-trust

SIS International Research (2018). *SMB Communications Pain Study White Paper.* [online]. Available at: https://www.sisinternational.com/smb-communications-pain-study-white-paper-uncovering-the-hidden-cost-of-communications-barriers-and-latency

StoryBrand (2018). *5 Questions That Will Make Any Talk Clear and Memorable.* [podcast] Building a StoryBrand with Donald Miller. Available at: https://itunes.apple.com/au/podcast/122-andy-stanley-5-questions-that-will-make-any-talk/id1092751338?i=1000423669340&mt=2

The Takeaway (2015). *Surprise! Why the Unexpected Feels Good, and Why It's Good For Us.* [online] Available at: https://www.wnyc.org/story/surprise-unexpected-why-it-feels-good-and-why-its-good-us/

Warren, R. (2008). *The Purpose Driven Life: What on Earth Am I Here For?* US: Zondervan.

Zak, P. (2014). *Why Your Brain Loves Good Storytelling.* [online] hbr.org. Available at: https://hbr.org/2014/10/why-your-brain-loves-good-storytelling

INDEX

LET'S CONTINUE THE CONVERSATION

This book is a beginning not an end. It's an invitation to begin a conversation that continues beyond the pages you hold in your hand. If you have found this book valuable in any way there are a number of ways to continue the conversation. I would love you to share your story with me. Whether it's a few lines or a few pages, I would be honoured to read how this book has impacted you or helped you become a better leader. You can email me directly at contact@shanemhatton.com.

I write regularly on leadership and communication as a helpful resource to an incredible tribe of people. You are invited to be a part of that tribe. You can join easily by visiting www.shanemhatton.com. There you will also find more information about my programs and ways we can do great work together. Finally, if this book has helped you, why not invest it into the life of a colleague, team member or friend and start a conversation with them.

I can't wait to continue the conversation with you.

ALSO BY SHANE HATTON

Packed with research-based insights from Australia's leading workplaces, *Let's Talk Culture* is the go-to how-to guide for people leaders who want to shape a world-class team culture by design.

**Published by and available from
Major Street Publishing.**